THE SECOND SCOTTISH
WARS OF INDEPENDENCE
1332-1363

THE SECOND SCOTTISH
WARS OF INDEPENDENCE
—— 1332-1363 ——

CHRIS BROWN

TEMPUS

First published 2002

PUBLISHED IN THE UNITED KINGDOM BY:

Tempus Publishing Ltd
The Mill, Brimscombe Port
Stroud, Gloucestershire GL5 2QG
Tel: 01453 883300
www.tempus-publishing.com

PUBLISHED IN THE UNITED STATES OF AMERICA BY:

Tempus Publishing Inc.
2 Cumberland Street
Charleston, SC 29401
Tel: 1-888-313-2665
www.tempuspublishing.com

British Library Cataloguing in Publication Data.
A catalogue record for this book is available from the British Library.

ISBN 0 7524 2312 6

Typesetting and origination by Tempus Publishing.
PRINTED AND BOUND IN GREAT BRITAIN.

CONTENTS

ACKNOWLEDGEMENTS

The debts incurred to one's friends and acquaintances in the course of writing a book comprise a list too long and tedious to inflict upon any reader, however I could not allow the opportunity to pass of publicly thanking some of the people whose help has been indispensable. Pride of place must go to my long-suffering wife Pat who has had to bear the burden of lengthy (tedious?) ramblings on the arms, tactics, strategy, politics and economics of late medieval Scotland as well as driving me around the country to examine battlefields and castles.

I would never have embarked on this project if I had not been admitted to St Andrews University to read for a doctorate in medieval history. I am particularly indebted to Dr Bill Knox, who proposed me for admittance in the first place; Dr Steven Boardman of Edinburgh University Scottish History Department who bravely provided me with an academic reference and Dr Hamish Scott whose belief in wider access to higher education made that admittance a reality. I might easily have fallen at the wayside without the guidance and support of my supervisor, Dr Michael Brown, who was kind enough to discuss this book with Jonathan Reeve at Tempus Publishing. I hope that their confidence has not been misplaced, but, sadly, I can blame no one but myself for any errors that have crept into this book.

Midlothian Library Service, particularly the Local Studies Unit at Loanhead and Penicuik Public Library have proved indefatigable in their efforts to procure me the material I needed: I cannot thank them enough.

Two Aberdeen University graduates have shaped my approach to history through half a lifetime of historical arguments. They are my parents: Rev Peter Brown RN (Retd.) and Mrs Margaret Brown. My only regret about this book is that my late father-in-law, Robert Smith, will never see it – I owe him more than I can say for his friendship and wisdom in the all too short period that I knew him.

For repeatedly rescuing me when I had done something unwise with the computer – including re-typing the entire manuscript at lightning speed – I am enormously indebted to my son, Robert.

Many friends and colleagues from my previous occupation as a concert lighting designer and contractor have given me encouragement in my change of career – they know who they are, but I must mention Paul Brown, Rob Maxtone-Graham, John Ramsay of EFX, Craig McMurdo and Derek Dick (better known as 'Fish'). To all of the above, *Slainthe Mhath*!

1

THE LION TRIUMPHANT?

The battle of Bannockburn in June 1314 is often seen as the concluding chapter of the Scottish War of Independence – King Robert's victory over the English confirming his own kingship and the liberty of the nation through a great feat of arms. In fact, the war would continue for another fifteen years before Scottish independence was acknowledged in the 'perpetual peace' of the treaty of 1328.

While the battle was a resounding demonstration of the power of Robert I, it was not sufficient to force his enemy to the negotiating table. The course of the war had steadily favoured the Scots for some time, but they were still a long way from complete victory. The defeat of Edward II's army prompted the surrender of some of the castles that held out against the Scots but several significant garrisons, particularly in the south-east where the English occupation had been more successful in gaining the acceptance of the community. Bannockburn did not win Robert's war, but it did strengthen his hand. The status conferred on him by victory over the English enhanced the prestige he had acquired through his successful campaigns in the Bruce/Balliol struggle for succession.

When Robert had himself made king at Scone Abbey in 1306 he could hardly be said to have had the wholehearted support of the community. The previous king of Scotland, John I, had abdicated in favour of Edward I of England, but he had done so only under duress. The internal opposition to the Bruce cause lay among those who refused to recognise the validity of John's abdication and therefore the legitimacy of Robert I's kingship. Robert was unquestionably usurping the Balliol dynasty in the view of a significant proportion of the community. Opposition to the Bruce dynasty tends to be seen as support for the English occupation. It was the aim of Bruce party propaganda that it should be seen in that light, and that aim was achieved more than adequately.

The strength of the Comyn family had been the mainstay of the Balliol party in the early years of the war against Edward I. However, any possibility of reconciling

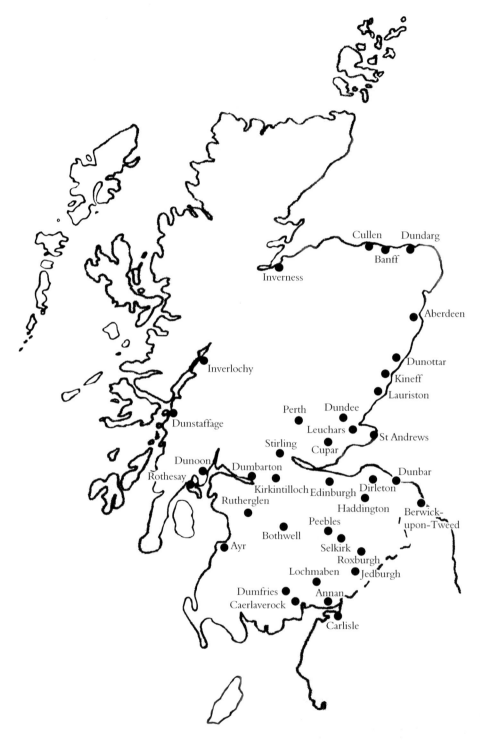

1. Significant towns and castles in Scotland.

the Comyns to a Bruce monarchy was lost in 1306 when Robert murdered the Comyn's leader, John, Lord of Badenoch, possibly because he was unable to secure his co-operation. The murder took place at the altar of the Whitefriars church at Dumfries, making Robert not only a killer, but a sacrilegious killer. This was offensive to medieval sensibilities and did the Bruce cause little good other than ensuring the removal of one of their most effective opponents. Indeed, the most immediate result was that Robert had to conduct an internal war against the powerful Comyn family and their allies while fighting the English.

The strength of Robert's position in the years after Bannockburn was very real; his military reputation was high, his authority was largely accepted throughout the population and his country was beginning to recover from the trials of the civil war and the occupation. Robert relied on the strength of a small coterie of men who had shown him devoted service over the years. He showed his appreciation to them in the traditional way of medieval monarchs. Settling land on a loyal servant did more than simply reward past service to the king, it gave the recipient a vested interest in continuing to give their support, not only to the present king, but, as we shall see, to his heirs.

The Parliament of 1315 had passed sentence of forfeiture on anyone with a claim on Scottish lands who had not yet made their peace with the king. King Robert was quite relaxed about these forfeitures insofar as a number of people were accepted into the king's peace and reinstated to at least some part of their property long after the deadline date, but he was more insistent on another provision of the act. In future, allegiance to the Scottish King must be absolute. Men would no longer be allowed to owe allegiance to the king of England if they wished to remain in the peace of the king of Scotland.

Since the invasion by Edward I in 1296, Scots who held lands in England and therefore owed service to English kings had been in a very difficult position. If Scottish resistance were in the ascendant, they would lose their English lands for treason to their liege lord if they joined the resistors or likewise have their Scottish lands ravaged if they declared for Edward. The threat of exclusion from their English properties has long been seen as evidence of a division in Scottish society between 'Normanised' or 'Anglo-Norman' nobles and their tenants. The oft-repeated assertion that the nobles of medieval Scotland were as much English as Scots and that the War of Independence was won by the yeoman classes despite the double-dealing of their lords and masters is untenable.

One of the oft-made comments about the Scottish aristocracy by English writers of the early fourteenth century was their unreliability. They might promise faithful service to the king of England, but were liable to re-join 'their own people' when pressed.

There were of course real divisions of loyalty. Some Scots maintained their allegiance to the Balliols, some stood by the fealty that they had given to Edward I after John's deposition, while some no doubt refused allegiance to Robert because he was an excommunicate or because they were simply horrified by the murder of John Comyn. Only a handful of Scottish nobles had significant landholdings in England. English manors might be an important part of a Scottish lord's estates, but they were never extensive enough to make that lord an important figure in English politics. This was not, in any case, simply a war of the aristocracy. The army of William Wallace had largely consisted of the common people when it fought at Stirling Bridge and Falkirk but then most large medieval armies consisted mainly of infantry and where could they be recruited from if not from the commons? In the early years of his struggle Robert had relied on troops recruited in the Western Isles, but as he gained control of more of the mainland he was able to call on the services of a greater part of the population.

This was a war of national communities and people were well aware of their nationality. Few people will fight unless there is a fairly obvious reason why they should do so. The willingness of Scottish people to continue the fight against the English despite many defeats indicates that although we may not fully understand their motivation they certainly felt strongly enough to risk life and limb in what seems to us a very hazardous undertaking.

The forfeitures of 1315 brought a new element into being that would affect the political condition of the country for the next forty years. Those who had suffered loss on account of their resistance to the Bruces had resisted for a variety of reasons, the blanket forfeiture gave them a common purpose – the recovery of their estates. Known to history as 'the Disinherited', they could only hope to restore their fortunes by displacing the Bruce dynasty in favour of the son of John I, Edward Balliol .

The first attempt to put this into effect was the De Soulis Conspiracy of 1320. This plan to assassinate Robert I failed miserably, but the conspirators must have thought that they had a good chance of pulling off a coup and of being able to establish Edward's kingship after Robert's death to have taken such a risk. As long as his kingship was not recognised by England, Robert's government would be at greater risk from internal threats. In order to secure his position he needed to extract more than just temporary truces from Edward II, he needed peace.

However, the victory at Bannockburn and the removal of English garrisons were not enough to end the war. Robert had to carry the war to the enemy if he wanted to achieve a political settlement that would acknowledge his kingship. The Scots had made occasional raids into the north of England under William Wallace and also under Bruce himself, but the scale of these operations was stepped up dramatically in the wake of the campaign of 1314. The counties of Westmoreland, Northumberland, Cumbria and Durham had born the brunt of the English war effort in Scotland for twenty years with their taxes, produce and manpower. With the focus of the war moving into the north of England these same communities were faced with destruction or accommodation; unable to resist militarily, they paid blackmail to King Robert's armies.

The Scots could afford to be high-handed in their dealings as long as they kept to their side of the bargain and refrained from indiscriminate destruction. If the communities thought they would be despoiled whether they paid or not there would have been little point in spending the money; they might as well fight. The ransoms of the most northerly parts of England were heavy, but the conditions attached to the truces, though not a burden in themselves, undermined the authority of the king of England. The ransom paid by the community included the right of the Scots to travel through that community unimpeded on their way to the next

2. Welsh infantryman. After Liver 'A'. PRO.

3. Irish infantryman. After Liver 'A'. PRO.

victim. Edward II could no longer offer 'good lordship' – peace, stability and security – to his subjects in the north. Yet Edward's unwillingness to come to terms with Robert remained steadfast even though he could not raise an army for a major attack on the Scots and several English raids into the border counties met with disaster at the hands of Douglas and Moray.

The Scots pressed further and further into England, but could make no impression on Edward. Edward was unmoved by defeat in Scotland and in the north of England, so Robert looked for another theatre where his enemy might be vulnerable, and identified Ireland as a possibility. The position of the English administration in Ireland was not completely secure, but there were no great threats to its general stability. The areas under English or English-affiliated control were reasonably settled and represented a useful resource to English monarchs in terms of revenue and manpower. Several Scottish lords had interests in Ireland already; the Bruces and Stewarts had held land in Ulster for some time, but the war with England undoubtedly denied them any profit from their possessions. Robert's invasion may have had the objective of returning these lands to Scottish nobles, but the primary goal was the destabilisation of the English community in Ireland. By encouraging the Irish to resist colonisation Robert hoped to draw English troops away from operations in Scotland. Continual campaigning in the borders was a strain on the communities that had to support the troops, but if Robert could move the focus of the war to Ireland, he could have a body of men continually exerting pressure on the English without the burden of feeding them from Scottish resources. The north of England had suffered so much from passing armies that it was becoming increasingly difficult to find much in the way of forage let alone booty anywhere north of the Tees.

Robert entrusted the Irish expedition to his brother Edward. Traditionally, historians have regarded Edward Bruce as headstrong or reckless, a view that is largely the product of the poet John Barbour, whose poem 'The Bruce' is the greatest account of medieval European kingship. In his verse biography of the king, Barbour tells us that Robert sent his brother to Ireland to keep him occupied. There is probably some degree of truth in this. The Scots had been defending themselves against the aggressive expansionism of the Plantagenets for twenty years, so inevitably there had been changes in Scottish society.

During the thirteenth century Scotland had enjoyed a peaceful relationship with her neighbour. The military operations of Alexander II and Alexander III were minor internal affairs; landowners may have owed service for their lands, but estates were valued more for their economic value than as a reservoir of manpower. Landlords and peasants alike owed forty days army service a year but they were seldom called upon to fulfil their obligations. The policies of Edward I and Edward II changed all this. Inevitably, a long war encourages the development of a military element in the community. For most people forty days service was undoubtedly an unwelcome distraction from farm or business, but for some soldiering became a full time occupation. The removal of those people from Scotland, where the community would have to support them, to Ireland, where they could support themselves from the land while still exerting military pressure on England had very practical attractions for King Robert.

4. Scottish infantryman. After Liver 'A', PRO.

Whether Robert approved of his brother's decision to make himself king of Ireland is open to question. Edward had already been recognised as the heir to the throne of Scotland, but at that time the king had no legitimate sons and his Queen, Elizabeth de Burgh, was a captive in England. When she returned to Scotland in the extensive prisoner exchange after Bannockburn the situation was changed. The king was still only in his early forties and could reasonably expect to father a son to inherit the crown. If Edward Bruce wanted to be a king he would have to look elsewhere to further his ambitions and Ireland looked like a good proposition.

The defeat and death of Edward at Faughart in 1318 brought about the collapse of the Scottish occupation. The invasion had been a failure in terms of conquest, but it had drawn the attentions of the English away from Scotland for three years and provided support for Robert's troops. Control of the northern part of the Irish Sea allowed Robert considerable freedom of movement. By forcing the enemy to accept a local truce in one area he could free up his troops and transport them to another theatre and repeat the process. Effectively, he had had an army embodied almost continually for several years.

The end of the war in Ireland brought the focus of operations back to the north of England but the Scots retained the initiative. The regular incursions of the Scots not only enriched the raiders; it impoverished the local communities. During the earlier years of the war, many of the nobility and gentry of Scotland, and particularly in Lothian and the border counties, had been faced with the choice of accepting the Edwardian occupation or losing their lands. Now the situation was reversed. The towns of northern England paid vast sums for 'protection', and English gentry found themselves obliged to make their own peace with the Scots in much the same way as their counterparts in Scotland had been doing for twenty years.

The operational nature of the war changed during this period. When Wallace raided into England he had led a large infantry force. He razed the areas he could reach, but the range of his force was obviously limited by their lack of mobility. King Robert's army was still infantry, but they travelled on horseback and dismounted to fight. The increased mobility of the Scots allowed Robert to extend the scope of his efforts; no town between the Humber and the Tyne could consider itself safe from extortion. Robert himself only led one raid after the close of the operations in Ireland. The rest of the operations were the province of Douglas and the Earl of Moray. The reputation that Douglas acquired would serve to frighten the children of northern England for generations, as 'The Black Douglas', the ultimate bogeyman.

Edward did not of course accept these Scottish incursions into his realm, but he could not maintain a standing army in the northern counties that could prevent them. He called for a tax of 2d in the mark (13s 4d) to pay for four captains and their troops, but the communities of the north made their own arrangements with the invaders, paying out vast sums to prevent their goods being stolen and their properties being destroyed. The activities of the Scots were disastrous for most people in the north of England, but for some the Scottish raids presented opportunities. Tynedale had been a possession of Scottish kings since the twelfth century. It was not an integral part of their realm, but a fief of the king of England that merely happened to be held – in the conventional feudal manner – by Scottish kings. The generally amicable nature of Anglo – Scottish relations during the thirteenth century and the concentration of

English rulers on their affairs in France had allowed Scottish kings to rule Tynedale as though it was part of their regal inheritance. As early as 1307, when Robert had first claimed the throne, the people of Tynedale had started to raid their neighbours; perhaps the Tynedale men genuinely saw themselves as subjects of the king of Scotland engaged in acts of war, but they had no real excuse to do so.

To exert further political pressure on Edward, Robert started to make grants of land in England to his followers in the same way as his English counterparts had rewarded the service of their retainers who had served in Scotland. Grants like these, whether made by Edward I or Robert I were only of any value as long as the military situation favoured the grantee. As the Scots recovered their country from the English, the titles granted by the Plantagenets became meaningless since the recipients could not exert their authority. The grants made by Robert in the north of England were probably never intended as a permanent fixture. They were political gambits challenging the ability of the English king to safeguard the interests of his own subjects, in the hope of forcing him to either recognise the ambitions of Robert or to offer battle.

Two general engagements were brought about through this policy, both of them clear victories for the Scots. The first of these was at Myton-on-Swale in Yorkshire. In September 1319 Edward II laid siege to Berwick. Unwilling to offer battle and concerned that the town would fall to the English, the Scots mounted an attack to draw Edward's forces back into England. The Archbishop of York, fulfilling his obligations as a northern magnate took command of the levies of Yorkshire and deployed them to obstruct the Scottish advance. The traditional mechanisms of local defence had not been called into play against invaders for a century, and the Archbishops army proved to be no match for the numerically inferior but immeasurably more effective Scots. The battle was superficially successful from Robert's point of view. The English had been beaten in a conventional battle and their army had been forced to raise its siege of Berwick. The prestige of Edward II was damaged and that of Robert greatly enhanced, but the Scots were no closer to a political settlement than they had been after Bannockburn.

In 1322 Robert mounted an unusually powerful expedition into England with the clear intention of rousing Edward to action. Edward's response was to strike into southern Scotland in the hopes of provoking the Scots into giving battle. He had recently defeated a rebellion led by Thomas of Lancaster, which perhaps given him confidence that he could reverse the trend of the war. His problem was that the Scots would not fight him unless they could do so in circumstances that would negate or at least offset the greater numbers of the English armies. Robert retired across the Forth conducting a 'scorched earth' policy in front of the advancing English. Unable to sustain his troops by foraging, Edward was forced to retire into England with nothing achieved. This time the Scots followed them and Edward himself narrowly avoided capture at Riveaulx Abbey after a sharp Scottish victory at Scawton. Unable to catch Edward, the Scots treated Yorkshire as they were treating Northumberland or Cumbria; that is, blackmailing communities and carrying off captives for ransom. Edward was fast losing control of the northern quarter of his country, but he was still not disposed to acknowledge Robert as king of Scotland. He may have been forced to entertain formal negotiations with people that he regarded as rebels against their leige lord, but he tried his utmost to avoid any mention at all of Robert.

5. Illuminated letter depicting the defence of Carlisle. Courtesy of Carlisle City Council.

6. Scots manning a catapult at the siege of Carlisle. Courtesy of Carlisle City Council.

Negotiations for a final settlement could not be successfully conducted without diplomatic recognition. Unable to pursue continual campaigns in the midlands of England, Robert could wring nothing more than another truce. It was supposed to last for thirteen years, though it seems unlikely that either king was confident that the truce would run its course. Beset by opposition at home, in Ireland and in France, Edward was hardly in a position to further his ambitions in Scotland, but he could try to limit the damage done to his prestige. King Robert was suffering from an unidentified illness – usually described as leprosy by contemporary English writers. The unity of his realm was not entirely dependent on his own strength and prestige, but there was internal opposition to the Bruce party. If Edward could outlive Robert without making any formal concessions to his *de facto* kingship, it might be easier for an alternative ruling house – the Balliols – to re-establish their kingship or for Edward (or his successors) to gain direct control over the Scots.

As it was, Edward did not last the pace. He lost control of his kingdom to his queen, Isabella of France and her lover, Roger Mortimer. They eventually found it expedient to 'do away' with Edward and replace him with his son, the fourteen-year-old Prince of Wales, now to be Edward III. The immediate consequence of Edward II's deposition was the end of the truce with Scotland. King Robert ordered a brief raid into England which nearly captured Norham castle before returning across the border. The Norham raid was a demonstration to Isabella and Mortimer that Robert was still intent on proving and making good his 'right'.

The new government was more preoccupied with making their own position secure than with relations with the Scots. Unable to respond immediately to Robert's challenge, they concluded indentures – fixed term contracts – with northern magnates to supply armed men for the defence of the realm. There was a flurry of military activity in England in the spring of 1327, but no campaign was initiated for several months. The spring preparations were probably undertaken for political purposes; to indicate that the English were still prepared to fight rather than make concessions to the Scots that would undermine the claims of the Plantagenets to power in Scotland. Isabella and Mortimer may have been looking for a diplomatic reaction, instead they provoked a new outbreak of hostilities in Ireland. King Robert's intervention in Ireland demanded a more positive strategy for the English. The mustering of troops was accelerated, and the young king, Edward III was despatched northwards to inspire his troops and defend his honour. The army that he nominally commanded was a large one. Soldiers were levied from all over England and a significant number of men-at-arms from Hainault joined the force. Robert did not respond to this challenge in person, entrusting his forces to Randolph and Douglas.

The superior mobility of the Scots allowed them to evade Edward's army in 'good' country and to seize advantageous terrain in poor country. For three miserable weeks in August and September the English army trailed after the Scots, unable to come to grips with them. No battle was fought during the Weardale campaign, but the Scots had certainly had the best of it. Indeed, Edward himself was lucky not to be captured by Douglas during a night attack on the English camp.

Edward's army disbanded, but the war was not over. Robert stepped up the pressure by continuing his raids into England, but now his operations were apparently becoming more permanent. In the autumn of 1327 it was believed that he was taking castles and building peels with a view to the permanent occupation of Northumberland. According to William Melton, Archbishop of York, Robert was making further land grants of English manors and villages to his knights, and 'confirming' the charters of English landholders.

The destruction of the northern counties could be sustained by the royal dignity for a while, but the permanent loss of territory could not. The English had profited by the acquisition of Berwick as a forward base for Scottish operations and Robert might derive the same value from capturing Carlisle or Newcastle. It had taken Robert ten years to liberate his kingdom from English occupation, it might take just as long for the English to remove Scottish garrisons from Northumberland and Cumbria. Though no great town had fallen to the Scots, it was only through good fortune.

However, Isabella and Mortimer ran out of options. They could not raise another army, the Weardale campaign had cost more than £70,000 – a massive sum for the early fourteenth century – and the treasury was empty. In any case, it would undoubtedly prove difficult to recruit the men even if the money was available – recent campaigns against the Scots were hardly an incentive to join the army. They had to negotiate with the Scots for a peace rather than a truce. Robert was a dying man and he was in a hurry to protect the inheritance of his son, David. A temporary suspension of conflict that did not accept his kingship would not be enough.

The terms that Robert demanded were not heavy. The unreserved acceptance of Scottish independence and the full sovereignty of Scottish kings was offset by a major financial payment, a 'contribution for peace', of £20,000 to the English exchequer – though in reality it seems that the money fell into the hands of Isabella and Mortimer. The treaty was confirmed by the marriage of Prince David of Scotland to Princess Joanna of England – the son of Robert I and the daughter of Edward II but neither Robert or his new 'friend and ally' Edward graced the wedding with their presence which was not a good omen.

A perpetual peace had been agreed, but how long would it last?

2
THE CAMPAIGN OF 1332

The final peace agreed in 1328 had been bought at a terrible price. Despite, or perhaps because of, the immense human cost, the treaty was desperately unpopular in England. Edward himself resented the 'shameful peace' which signed away the rather self-ordained 'right' of his grandfather, Edward I, to the feudal overlordship of Scotland, and was inclined to disavow the treaty on the grounds that he was a minor when it was concluded. His was not the only resentment. The return of the Scottish coronation stone had been prevented by a mob of Londoners angry at the 'loss' of Scotland and there was opposition among the aristocracy, particularly those who considered that they had claims to Scottish estates by virtue of charters that had been made in their favour by Edward I.

Some of the Scottish and English lords who had lost their lands in either country during the war had been reinstated, but the majority of them had not. During the regency of Isabella, these lords – the Disinherited – could only kick their heels and wait for change. Isabella had more than enough problems of her own to contend with without stirring up any further trouble with the Scots, so she chose not to press their case, initially for fear of losing the 'contribution' money that the Scots were paying as part of the provisions of the 1328 treaty. Once the payments had been completed Isabella could perhaps have adopted a more positive attitude to their claims, but by then it was too late, the Disinherited had turned to Edward. Edward had come to the throne as a minor, but he was growing up. His mother's regency could not last indefinitely and forward-looking members of the political class were starting to align themselves with the young king. When he asserted his authority with a successful coup in October 1330, two of the most influential disinherited lords, Beaumont and Wake, were already firm members of his party. There was of course a price for such support, and Edward was willing to pay it in the hope that there would be rewards for himself in the future. What he was not willing to do was to embark on an immediate campaign to recover lands for these wars, at least until the final instalment of the contribution had been made.

Mindful of his own disastrous campaign against the Scots in 1327, Edward was unwilling to infringe the treaty of 1328 openly, but he could turn a blind eye to the activities of others or claim that he was powerless to prevent them.

That is exactly what he did. After the Scots had paid the final instalment of the 'contribution' in the summer of 1331, Edward could afford to take a more aggressive stance with the Scots, but was still not prepared to provoke the Scottish Guardian, Thomas Randolph, the Earl of Moray. As long as Randolph was alive he could wield the prestige of King Robert and unite the kingdom to effectively resist invasion. Randolph's reputation as a commander was awesome, but he would not live forever. Realising that there was little hope of a diplomatic solution, and no doubt perfectly aware of Edward III's duplicitous attitude, Randolph took measures for the defence of the country.

While Edward played for time with Scottish emissaries, Beaumont started to recruit an army. The aim of this expedition was to put Edward Balliol – son of King John I – on the Scottish throne in place of David Bruce. Balliol had spent most of his life on his family's estate in Picardy, where his father had spent his declining years after he had been released from the captivity in England that followed his forced abdication in 1296. John had been liberated due to papal intervention to what was effectively house-arrest in the care of the king of France. John had been deposed and imprisoned, but the Scots who had continued to fight Edward I until 1304 had done so behalf of their exiled king. In 1302/03 the restoration of the Balliol monarchy had begun to look like a real possibility, suggesting that the Balliol cause was not completely lost. Edward Balliol and his supporters – including Edward III who had granted him safe-conducts and financial support – were hoping to exploit latent sympathy for the late king John as well as hostility to the Bruce family.

The men that enlisted in the army that gathered on the Humber recognised Edward Balliol as king of Scotland, but Henry Beaumont, who had served in the Bannockburn and Weardale campaigns probably had real command of the project. They were all taking considerable risks in participating, but the potential rewards were vast. Beaumont himself claimed the earldom of Buchan and Thomas Wake of Liddel hoped to obtain the barony of Kirkandrews and the lordship of Liddesdale. They were joined by Beaumont's son-in-law David de Strathbogie, claimant to the earldom of Atholl and Gilbert d'Umfraville, claimant to the earldom of Angus.

Not all of the people who joined the camp of the Disinherited at their camp on the Humber had such ambitious aims. Small freeholders who had lost their lands through their attachment to the Balliol cause, some of whom had been receiving small pensions from English kings, could only hope to restore their fortunes through their adherence to more prominent members of the Disinherited and the destruction of the Bruce administration. Obviously, this was a very small group from which to recruit an army. It is hard to believe that the

Opposite   7. A fourteenth-century man-at-arms.

8. A fourteenth-century light infantryman: Scots, English, Irish, Welsh or French troops would have appeared much the same.

Disinherited did not expect to receive aid from people in Scotland whose loyalty to the Bruce family had been dependant on the strong government of Robert I, or who hoped for preferment under a new government that would be grateful for their support.

In the summer of 1332 the army of the Disinherited was waiting for the optimum moment to make their attack. Thomas Randolph, the last of Robert's lieutenants and the Guardian of the Realm since the death of the old king in 1329, was failing fast and the Disinherited were ready to move as soon as they heard of his death on the 20 July. They embarked in a fleet of more than eighty vessels from Hull on 31 July. A week later they landed at Kinghorn in Fife where they were confronted by a Scottish force under the Earl of Fife. Undeterred, the invaders disembarked a party of archers and spearmen with men-at-arms in support and secured a beachhead where they could unload their stores before marching on Dunfermline.

Aware of the impending attack, but without any information to indicate whether it would fall north or south of the Forth, only that it would take place somewhere on the eastern seaboard, the Scots had raised two armies to repel the invaders. One force was recruited in the northern counties and commanded by the Earl of Mar and the other was raised in the south under the Earl of March. The Balliol party had to act quickly if they were going to be able to seize the reins of government. As long as there were strong Bruce forces in the field they could not hope to enlist much local support. Eager to prevent a conjunction of the two Scottish forces, the leaders of the Disinherited chose the boldest possible course of action. Rather than take up a defensive position and wait for the Scots appear, Beaumont and Balliol led their army toward a large body of Scottish troops under the Earl of Mar that was camped on the high north bank of the river Earn. From their elevated position the Scots could see that they outnumbered Balliol's army camped at the 'miller's acre' near the hamlet of Forteviot.

Guided by a Scottish Knight, apparently Sir Andrew Murray of Tullibardine who was later executed for treason, Balliol's force crossed the river and made an attack on the Scots under cover of darkness. Thinking that they had engaged and defeated the Scottish men-at-arms, the invaders re-grouped around a burning house, only to be informed that another Scottish force was approaching. The bulk of Mar's army had not been damaged in the night attack – many of them had spent the night carousing – and they were now deploying for battle. The Balliol army could hardly avoid battle, but they were very heavily outnumbered and some of them at least had been in action through the night. The whole Balliol army probably comprised about 1500 to 2000 men, far fewer than the Scots, but they had the advantage of being a professional operation. The leadership largely consisted of experienced commanders, the force had been in being for some months, and it undoubtedly included a large proportion of experienced troops who had served in Scotland or France in the past.

The Scottish army had been raised very quickly and their leaders were inexperienced compared to men like Henry Beaumont. Confident of an easy victory through superior numbers and encouraged by the string of military successes that the Scots had enjoyed under the leadership of Robert I, Moray and

Douglas in the years following Bannockburn the Scots were more than willing to attack. The first Scottish assault may have only comprised a few hundred men-at-arms, the personal followings of Lord Robert Bruce (an illegitimate son of Robert I and perhaps embittered by his exclusion from any share of regal power), the Earl of Menteith and the new Earl of Moray, son of the late Guardian.

Logically, the Scots should have been able to crush Balliol's army with ease, which would in all probability have been the end of the entire business. Edward III would have been unlikely to allow a second attempt to be mounted from England even if Edward Balliol and his chief supporters had been able to escape the battle with their lives. However, there were serious divisions among the Scottish commanders. Angered perhaps that he had not been given sole command of the army, lord Robert Bruce quarrelled with Mar, accusing him of cowardice and collusion with the enemy. Mar had spent much of his early life as a captive in England and was sensitive to suspicions that he might have been too friendly with his captors. Mar had certainly had some involvement with the Disinherited and may well have had some sympathy for their predicament, he had been an exile himself for much of his life, but there seems to have been no justification whatsoever for Bruce's accusations beyond personal animosity.

Furious with one another and determined to demonstrate their patriotism, Mar and Bruce returned to their respective divisions and prepared to advance. The invaders had deployed at the head of a narrow glen, presumably in order to offset the disparity in numbers by limiting the number of Scots who could come to blows at any one time. As the Scots drew nearer to their enemies the novel tactics of their opponents started to become apparent. The Scots relied entirely on the strength of spearmen in close order, apparently making no use at all of archers and perfectly confident that they would be able to overwhelm the enemy in a simple direct advance, much as their forbears had done at Myton or Bannockburn. Balliol's force included a high proportion of archers deployed as an integral part of the army's structure for battle. In order to maximise the effectiveness of their firepower, Beaumont had deployed his force on a narrow front, probably less than 300 yards, with his archers on the wings of the formation. They had been instructed to concentrate on the flanks of the approaching Scots thus funnelling them toward the men-at-arms in the centre of the Balliol line. By the time the Scots reached that line their ranks were in disarray, but they were making progress when matters took a turn for the worse as the Earl of Mar led his division into the fray.

The battlefield was already too constricted for the first formation to be able to fight effectively; Mar's force pressed in on the rear of the preceding formation and completely disrupted it. Unable to manoeuvre, the close-packed spearmen and men-at-arms lost their momentum as well as their formation and turned into a vulnerable and confused mob. The faltering Scots were now at the mercy of the invaders. Beaumont and Balliol roused their troops to make one more effort and the Scots finally broke and ran; their casualties so heavy, according to the chronicler John Fordoun, that they formed a pile as tall as a spear. The Earl of Fife tried to lead an orderly withdrawal but there was no real hope of regrouping his troops in the face of the Balliol army, whose men-at-arms now took to their horses and made

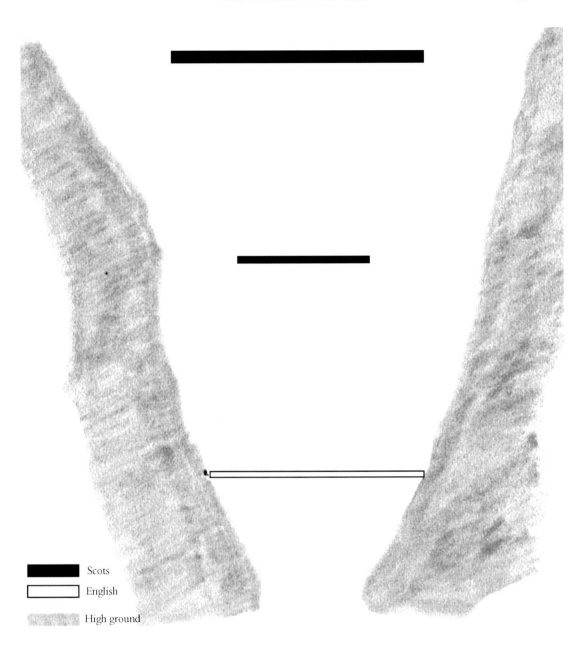

Scots

English

High ground

9. DUPPLIN MUIR, 11 AUGUST 1332

The army of Edward Balliol, consisting largely of English men-at-arms and archers, deployed across a narrow glen to protect their flanks. The leading Scottish formation was exposed to the full power of the English archers but managed to maintain good order. They were making progress when the second Scottish formation joined the fight causing confusion among the Scots who were already engaged. This was compounded by the heavy casualties in the Scottish leadership and allowed Balliol to achieve a dramatic victory. However, he could not mobilise enough support to convert his battlefield triumph into a favourable political settlement. Author illustration.

10. Edward Balliol's army camped in this valley on the night before the battle of Dupplin Muir.

a vigorous pursuit. Fife himself was taken prisoner in the confusion.

The Scots suffered a large number of casualties, a number of earls and barons were killed including the Earl of Moray and the earls of Mar and Menteith. The climax of the battle had been a bitter struggle at close quarters, but Balliol's – or Beaumont's – victory had been made possible by the archers. The longbow did not make its first appearance on the battlefield at Dupplin Muir. Indeed, archery had been crucial to the English victory at Falkirk in 1297 and again at the battle of Boroughbridge in 1322, but this was the first of the longbow victories that help define our perception of the Hundred Years War.

Edward's own casualties had been light, but not negligible. His archers and spearmen were largely unscathed, but in any case could probably be recruited reasonably easily locally or from England as long as he had the money to pay wages. The thirty or forty men-at-arms killed on the battlefield, plus however many had been temporarily or permanently put out of action by wounds, were more of a problem. Many of the troops that had taken part in the expedition would want to return to their homes in England and the remainder had their own estates to recover. Too much of the Scottish aristocracy had Bruce connections and too much of the gentry were attached to that aristocracy for casualties among the knights and the men-at-arms to be readily replaced by defectors from the Bruce party.

The disinherited made their way to Perth and set about trying to make the town defensible as a base for their future operations. Perth had some defences already and the Balliol army repaired these 'old works' with palisades, but it could hardly be described as a walled city. Balliol had gained a breathing space, but he was hardly secure.

The second Scottish army, under the Earl of March was still intact. The only obvious course for March to pursue was to contain the Balliol party, so he too led his troops to Perth and settled down to a siege of the town. March was unable to inspire his force to storm the town despite superior numbers, and no great efforts were undertaken to reduce the defences. After a week of little or no activity, March learnt that a Scottish naval force under the Flemish mercenary, John Crabbe, had attacked the Balliol fleet at the mouth of the river Tay and had been beaten off with severe losses. With this news, the earl's army disbanded, unable to find the necessary supplies to feed itself and unwilling to engage the enemy.

While Balliol was trying to secure his position in Perth, war broke out in Galloway. Families with a tradition of loyalty to the Balliol cause had started to raid their Bruce party neighbours under the leadership of Sir Eustace Maxwell. The Bruce party could not ignore this development if they were to be able to depict themselves as the 'proper' government and the Balliol party as interlopers. The new Guardian of Scotland – Sir Andrew Moray; a wealthy lord with landed interests in several parts of the country – led troops into the south-west to repair the situation.

When the Scots decamped from Perth Edward Balliol looked like a man whose ship had come in. His forces had given him a dramatic victory that had recovered a cause that had seemed hopeless for decades, there was no enemy army of any consequence in the field and a popular rising had started in his favour in Galloway. Triumph on the battlefield was most welcome, but if Edward wanted to be king he would have to gain acceptance from a larger potion of the society than could be supplied by the Disinherited. The more public recognition of his kingship he could extract from outside his immediate entourage, the more credible and acceptable he would become to the large part of the population whose chief ambition was a quiet life.

First, as a new king, it was imperative for him to be crowned. The act of coronation itself would furnish him with a modest degree of status among the credulous but the real value of the exercise lay in being able to impose attendance on influential and powerful individuals. The attendance of many magnates and lords at Edward's coronation – enforced or not – would have been an endorsement of his right to rule, so the absence of virtually all of them did not bode well for the future of the Balliol party.

Edward might be crowned, but he had still to win the country. The deaths of so many members of the senior Scottish aristocracy at Dupplin Muir had weakened the leadership of the Bruce party but not destroyed it. The death or capture of one Bruce party leader might lead to a succession struggle between magnates, but not to the extinction of the cause. If the heir to a Bruce sympathiser was to make good their inheritance they would generally have to do so through the success of the Bruce party. An accommodation with the Balliol party would almost inevitably require denying the claims of one or more members of the Disinherited.

Despite this, as the summer progressed, fortune continued to favour the Balliol cause. Edward was able to take a force into the south-west through Cunningham and Kyle and achieve dominance over the Bruces in Galloway before moving to the south-east. Anxious to establish his authority as widely and as quickly as possible, Edward made his headquarters at Roxburgh. The Scots under Sir Andrew Moray could not raise enough men to fight Edward Balliol and he could not commit enough men to force battle on the Scots. Balliol had won the crown through the inordinate success of a relatively small force, he could lose it again just as easily unless he could establish his kingship quickly. He could not afford a lengthy stalemate, but needed to press home his current advantage to prevent a Bruce recovery.

Moray kept Edward under observation, looking for an opportunity to strike. Believing that Edward had left the bulk of his troops in Roxburgh and taken up quarters at Kelso Abbey on the other side of the river Tweed, Sir Andrew tried to sever communications between the two by seizing and destroying the only bridge. The operation failed completely and Sir Andrew was taken prisoner. Edward had beaten his enemy – again – which was important to his prestige and the Bruce party had lost its leader – again.

However, the Scots were not completely overwhelmed by these events. The Earl of Fife, captured at Dupplin Muir, had been induced to throw in his lot with the invaders. Given that there was an army on his doorstep and that he was in custody himself he perhaps did not have much choice. Edward committed the town of Perth to the earl's care before he set out for Galloway, and was probably unsurprised when it fell to the Scots on 7 October 1332. The Earl of Fife was a strange choice of keeper but Edward did not have much choice when making the appointment. The other members of the expedition might have been more reliable, but they each had their own projects to pursue. If Henry Beaumont was to make good his claim to the earldom of Buchan or David Strathbogie was to acquire the earldom of Atholl, they would have to base themselves in those areas. They would have to maintain a visible presence powerful enough to establish their own authority as provincial leaders and to physically exclude their opposite numbers in the Bruce party. As a defector from the Bruce party, the Earl of Fife already enjoyed possession of his lands and did not have to fight a campaign to acquire them. Edward may well have preferred one of his more established supporters, but he could not spare one and could not possibly leave the town undefended – that would imply that he had no confidence in his own cause. Better – apparently – to have his trust and favour betrayed than to simply abandon one of the most important towns in the country.

Edward Balliol had made considerable progress in his cause, but he had done so with the help of others, and they needed to be rewarded for their efforts. The more prominent members of the Disinherited had risked wealth and wellbeing to win huge estates, but his most important supporter had not yet become officially involved in any way.

Edward III had studiously refused to take any notice of the Balliol expedition before it left England and for a brief period chose to regard the outbreak of war as an internal Scottish problem. However, Balliol would not have been able to mount his expedition without the help of the English king, the price of which was acknowledged by Balliol in November 1332. Balliol would recognise the king of

England as his feudal superior for his kingdom of Scotland – the relationship that Edward I had imposed on John I in 1291. Yet, for all his aid, Edward expected more than the restoration of his grandfather's claims of overlordship. Edward was to receive 2000 librates of land in parts of Scotland adjacent to England, but that was such a vast area that effectively almost the whole of southern Scotland was to be annexed to the English crown in perpetuity. Edward Balliol was not simply to be the agent of Edward III; although he was perfectly happy to be a vassal king, he was also serious about the 'king' part of the equation.

Nonetheless Edward III did hope to achieve political suzerainty over Scotland and possession of a lot of southern Scotland through the offices of Edward Balliol, and it is important to remember that the war that commenced with the Dupplin Muir campaign was never simply a dynastic struggle between the Bruce and Balliol parties. Certainly it was a civil war in the sense that Scots fought on both sides, but Edward Balliol was never in any sense independent of English support. Without the money and men supplied by Edward III he would never have been in a position to mount his first campaign. The 'international' nature of the war was certainly clear to contemporary opinion. The *Lanercost Chronicle* invariably refers to the Bruce party as 'the Scots', despite consistently describing Edward Balliol as the king of Scotland, and *Scalacronica*, written by Sir Thomas Grey, a Northumbrian knight who actually served in the war, is always perfectly clear that one side in the war is 'the English' and the other side is 'the Scots', although he too refers to Edward Balliol as king. When Grey writes of 'the English' he may be referring to the actions of Scottish men in the service of Edward III or Edward Balliol, but they are still 'English' as far as he is concerned. The Scottish chronicler John of Fordoun takes a similar stance.

Balliol was never independent of Edward III, but he was not going to be a puppet either. He had no intention of simply abandoning the entirety of southern Scotland; he was going to have the 2000 librates carefully measured by his own appointees, rather than estimated by Edward III's officers. Yet before this survey could be made the war took a turn for the worse for the Balliol party. There seems to have been little activity on either side after the capture of Moray, and a truce may have been made with a view to finding a peaceful, constitutional settlement at a Parliament to be attended by both parties. Balliol left Roxburgh in December and made his way to Annan in the south-west. While there, he received the Earl of Carrick, nephew of the late king, into his peace. The acceptance of the Balliol cause by such a prominent member of the Bruce party must have seemed a political godsend for Edward. The weakness of the Disinherited lay primarily in their inability to mobilise enough support among the great landowners that had *not* been disinherited, so any recruit from their ranks would be a boost to the morale of the new government.

However, Carrick's defection was short-lived. The son of the late guardian – John Randolph, Earl of Moray and Robert the Steward, had gathered a force at Moffat and made a dawn attack on Edward Balliol. Edward had either allowed his English supporters to go home, assuming that he had won his war, or, more credibly, they had come to the end of their contracts and Edward did not have the money to pay them even if they could be persuaded to extend their service. Such

11. A fourteenth-century archer.

support as Edward had been able to draw to him among the Scots was not enough to offset the loss of his English troops, and he was lucky to escape unscathed. He fared better than some of his followers, including his younger brother and only heir, Henry, who was killed in the fighting. Edward then made his way to Carlisle and immediately started to petition Edward III for military and financial aid for a second attempt at gaining the Scottish crown. The Earl of Carrick, freed from the constraint of having the small but powerful Balliol force ensconced in his locality, resumed his allegiance to King David.

With Balliol out of the way, the Bruce party was able to regain control of the country quickly. The functions of government – taxation and justice – were re-established effectively and the crown revenues were accounted formally at an exchequer audit in February 1333, just two months after the expulsion of Edward Balliol.

A new Guardian had been appointed to replace Sir Andrew Moray: Archibald Douglas, brother of the famous Sir James Douglas. Sir Archibald was faced with the likelihood that Edward Balliol would return, this time with the overt and unstinting support of Edward III. The practice of the Scots under King Robert had been to avoid general engagements and to demolish castles to deny them to the enemy, but he had made an exception of Berwick. The economic importance of Berwick made it a desirable possession for Scottish and English kings alike, but it also had considerable political significance. In the previous war, King Robert had struggled assiduously to recover the town and castle from the English, but he did not demolish the castle or the town walls as he did elsewhere. Instead he chose to establish a garrison and invested heavily in the fortifications. If the old king had thought that investment worthwhile, no Guardian could afford to abandon Berwick without a fight.

By the end of March 1333 Berwick was under siege by the forces of Edward Balliol and a group of English magnates. The magnates were each ostensibly operating as private individuals and without the sanction of Edward, but if he had disapproved of their actions he would almost certainly have put a stop to them. There can be little doubt that Edward was fully aware of their activities and that the siege of Berwick had his whole-hearted yet tacit support. Edward's official position was that the conflict in Scotland was a matter for the Scots and nothing to do with him, however any Scottish military activity in the rear of Edward Balliol's army would inevitably entail Scottish troops entering England, and that would obviously be an act of war. That this does not seem to have been considered an issue by the Scots would indicate that they, at least, were well aware that what they were conducting was not a civil war. They evidently believed that Edward III was already effectively at war with them, so crossing the border and making the English king become formally involved was not going to make matters any worse than they were already.

Rather than force a battle to raise the siege, Douglas undertook two raids into the north of England hoping to draw the English forces back into Northumberland and thereby relieving Berwick. Neither of Douglas' raids achieved their objective but they did serve Edward III's purposes very well. The Scots had, in his view, broken an existing peace and he was now free to take up arms on his own account or on behalf of his vassal if he saw fit. Edward

12. Perhaps the sole priority of the medieval soldier - money.

summoned his parliament, ostensibly for counsel on the Scottish situation, but really in the hope that parliament would provide the money to fund his expansionist policies. Parliament was not as co-operative as he might have hoped and refused to sanction taxation for a war against the Scots. Edward would have to rely on contracts (or indentures) with his magnates and a questionable application of the royal prerogative to raise troops and the money to feed them and pay them if he was going to fight.

Edward had not totally abandoned the idea of acquiring the throne of Scotland for himself through the resurrected claims of his grandfather, but the refusal of his Parliament to support his ambition forced him to attempt the control of Scotland through a client King, and Edward Balliol was the only viable candidate.

3

THE SIEGE OF BERWICK AND
THE BATTLE OF HALIDON HILL

When Edward III started to support the Balliol cause he did so at arms length so that he could deny any responsibility if things went wrong for the Disinherited. Things had indeed gone wrong, but the apparent near-success of Edward Balliol suggested that the matter was worth pursuing further. The English parliament had refused to countenance an attempted conquest of Scotland, but that did not prevent Edward from supporting his vassals or from raising troops on his own initiative; it merely prevented him levying taxation to pay for it. As early as January 1333 he had started to make preparations for the campaign that he would have to fight in Scotland if his vassal – Edward Balliol – was to be made king of Scots under Edward's feudal superiority.

By diverting revenue from the exchequer to a temporary war treasury at York, Edward was able to lay his hands on money for his operations without causing conflict with Parliament. Large sums were paid out to the Disinherited lords that had returned to England after Edward Balliol was ousted and more was given to English lords who would supply troops for Edward II's own campaign. In February he made arrangements to move the centre of his administration from London to York to ease communications for the duration of his Scottish war. Edward may have expected this to be a temporary measure, but York remained his 'capital' for the next five years because of his inability to conclude his offensives successfully.

By April 1333 Edward's intentions had become quite plain. His administrators had been forwarding supplies – particularly wheat and oats – to Newcastle, where extra grain storage had to be requisitioned from local merchants before another influx of produce which had been demanded from counties in the midlands and south of England. The transport of this materiel to Newcastle was obviously an issue. The seaports of eastern England were called upon to provide ships for the purpose, but the demands were so great that plans to raise a fleet of warships had to be severely curtailed because of the lack of available vessels. The possibility of French raids on the English coast was an issue that could not be ignored either, so Edward's naval resources were stretched to the limit for the campaign season of 1333.

13. A Scottish medieval galley.

When Edward III reached Berwick the town had already been under siege for two months. The underground water conduits that the townspeople and garrison depended on had been uncovered during the construction of earthworks around the town but the defenders were still determined to resist. This was a dangerous course of action for the inhabitants. When Berwick had been captured by Edward I in 1296 he had burned the town to the ground and murdered so many of the townspeople – 7000 according to chronicle accounts – that English clergy had been moved to petition him to end the slaughter.

While the Scottish army under Douglas carried fire and sword through Northumberland, the English king stood firm at Berwick, refusing to be distracted from his immediate tactical objective. He was prepared to offer battle to decide the future of Berwick, but he was not prepared to chase after the Scots in the hope of forcing an engagement with no obvious goal. He pressed on with the siege, ordering up equipment from York.

The most important siege ordnance was still kinetically powered – catapults and trebuchet – but the firearm was beginning to appear on the battlefields of Europe. A gunpowder weapon of some description had been used during the Weardale campaign of 1327, but seems to have made no impact on warfare other than to be mentioned as a curiosity by the poet Barbour. The use of gunpowder does not necessarily imply the existence of guns, however. An earthenware pot filled with gunpowder and stones and with a match fuse would make a potent weapon when cast from a catapult, though the risk of premature detonation would be high. The chronicle record of firearms or 'bombs' at Berwick is supplemented, if not quite confirmed, by the fact that Edward III paid for the chief ingredients of gunpowder – saltpetre and sulphur – to be brought to Berwick from York.

Regardless of the nature of the English siege artillery it seems to have been fairly effective. The castle and town were both severely damaged, but Edward could not cause a breach in the town wall sufficient enough to allow entry for a storming party. He seems to have been content to reduce the town through starvation and bombardment, but he did not hold back from ordering assaults. One of these was a sea-borne attack. At high tide ships approached the walls of the town to land troops and the Scots only managed to repel the attack through good fortune. They used burning faggots against the highly combustible wooden ships of the enemy, a device which backfired when the defenders managed to set fire to buildings in the town. A truce was arranged while they dealt with the flames. Once the fires had been doused the defenders seem to have reneged on an agreement to surrender the town, but Edward was prepared to grant a new truce

No town or castle could withstand a close siege indefinitely, and the defenders, short of food and water, would have to seek terms from Edward sooner or later if they were not relieved. The compact eventually agreed was complex, allowing for a variety of situations that might possibly arise and carefully describing which of these possibilities would constitute relief of the garrison and which would bring about its surrender. The truce was to last for fifteen days to give the defenders time to inform Douglas, currently campaigning in southern Northumberland, of their situation.

Edward was determined to avoid a repeat of his Weardale campaign, and Edward Balliol's siege of Berwick gave him an excellent opportunity to force his enemy to come to him both strategically and tactically. The Guardian was under pressure to save the town and had failed to draw the English army away from Berwick through his diversionary operations in the north of England. Edward wanted battle on his own terms and the Guardian was forced to offer it by the deterioration of the town's garrison. Edward gave safe conducts to members of the garrison so that they could seek out Douglas and explain the situation to him, but he had taken hostages as security that the Scots would not default on their promises. Edward started to hang hostages and the garrison commander – the Earl of March – was aware that the strong morale of the inhabitants could not be expected to survive long if people could see their friends or relatives being executed in the enemy lines. With no operations in hand that would affect Edward's ability to continue the siege, Douglas had no option but to fight in circumstances that favoured the English, who could now choose the ground that they would fight on. The Scots believed that their army was considerably larger than Edward's force, and that they had the upper hand. The example of the disastrous battle of Dupplin Muir less than a year previously must have made some impression on them because they did not immediately approach the English army to offer battle, but the fact that they raised a large army indicates that they had not ruled out the possibility of a general

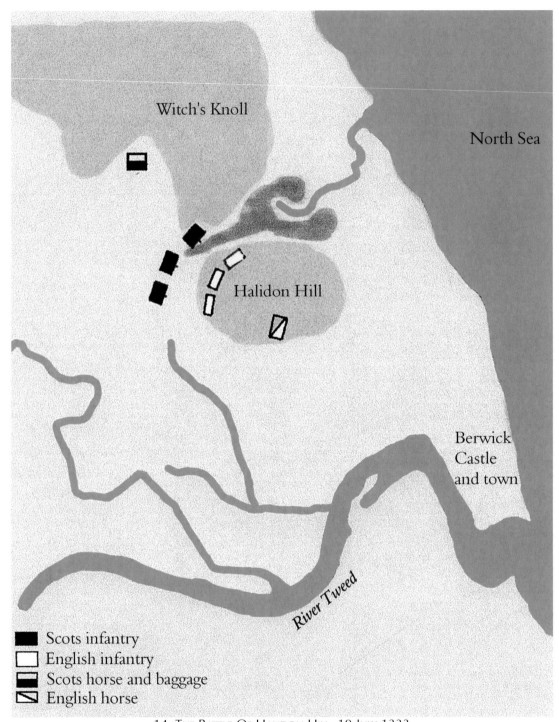

14. The Battle Of Halidon Hill, 19 July 1333

Having failed to draw the English army away from its siege of Berwick by raiding Northumberland, Lord Douglas either had to accept the loss of the town or offer battle. Leaving their horses at the foot of Witch's Hill, the Scots made a direct, frontal approach on the English position. Edward's army was perfectly deployed to deal with just such an attack and could not be outflanked. Author illustration.

engagement. If Douglas had been intent on a raiding operation a smaller and more mobile force would have been more appropriate.

There is no useful information concerning the size of either army. No wardrobe book exists for the campaign of 1333, which would have given us some insight into the military mobilisation of Edward III's household and no indentures with lords or contractors have survived. The practice of making estimates of army strengths in one year on the basis of information pertaining to a different campaign is a dangerous one. The forces raised by Edward for his Scottish war varied enormously from year to year depending on his other military commitments, his financial situation, and the nature of the campaign in progress. The presence of a greater number of senior nobles than in subsequent years should not be taken as an indication that the army of 1333 was necessarily larger than its successors, and it would seem that both sides believed the Scots to have the greater numbers.

Douglas was forced to take the offensive strategically in order to attempt the relief of the town, but he was also obliged to take an attacking stance tactically. Even if he had been able to execute an advance on the town successfully he would not have particularly improved the tactical position. The presence of a greatly enlarged force within the town would only have exacerbated the logistical problems that any besieged garrison would face. Edward deployed his army on Halidon Hill in three divisions of men-at-arms and spearmen, each division flanked by archers, a pattern that was followed by the English for the next century. The right-hand formation was commanded by Sir Edward Bohun, the left by Edward Balliol and the centre by King Edward himself. Their position at Halidon gave them dominance over the locality. The Scottish army could only approach Berwick at the risk of exposing their flank to attack, so Douglas was obliged to attack the English or abandon the town.

Douglas also divided his army into three formations. The truce arranged between Edward II and the town was due to come to an end that night, so Douglas did not have the time for a battle of manoeuvre even if he had the inclination. One of the provisions of the truce was that a force of 200 men-at-arms from the Scottish army entering the town would constitute a technical relief. This did not imply that the siege would be lifted if the force entered the town, but that the garrison of the town would not have to surrender under the terms of the truce. Douglas detailed a force to attempt an entry and Edward III made dispositions to prevent it but the arrangement came to nothing. The result of the battle would have made this provision redundant in any case; a Scottish victory would have removed the threat to the town and an English victory would have left the garrison just as isolated as it had been before the truce was made.

Given the outcome of the battle of Dupplin Muir just a few months before, the choice of a frontal attack seems positively suicidal, but it is always questionable to compare one battle with another. It is only reasonable to assume that the Scottish leadership at the time did not consider that the tactical situation at Halidon was the same as the one at Dupplin or they would have behaved differently. No one sets out to lose a battle after all. In what sense they believed the situations to be different is impossible to identify at this distance and they may have adopted a tactical practice at the second battle that was never documented, or if it was the document has not survived. Although the battle of Dupplin Muir had been greatly influenced by the force of longbowmen that comprised a considerable proportion of the English army and their Balliol party allies, the fight had been concluded by the close-quarter melee typical of medieval actions. The Scots command may have decided that their best chance of victory lay in developing their attack as quickly as possible in order to exclude the English archers from effective participation before the arrow storm could take its toll on the Scottish formations. Alternatively, they may have considered Dupplin Muir to be a fluke and not indicative of a viable tactical development. In any case, Douglas had no real choice; any attempt to approach the English flanks would only result in a re-alignment of their army – the Scots would still have to attack up a steep hill.

The Scots had taken up a position on rising ground about three miles from Berwick and facing toward the English army. Edward had no intention of leaving his advantageous position to engage the Scots, so Douglas was obliged to attack if he wanted to save Berwick from being captured. The path of their advance took them down the slope and across a marsh – the farm in between the two armies is still called Bogend – which the Scots had to negotiate before attempting to move uphill toward the English. If Douglas thought that a precipitate attack was the best option, he had chosen the wrong place to try to put it into practice. The lengthy approach uphill after negotiating soft ground must have exhausted his troops before they even came to blows. When they did contact the enemy they had to press the fight uphill, a huge disadvantage in hand-to-hand combat.

This was exactly what Edward had hoped and planned for. The Scots, already tired by their advance, were now subjected to hails of arrows, inflicting many casualties and, perhaps more crucially, seriously disrupting their closely ordered ranks.

The first contact occurred between the division of Edward Balliol and that of the Earl of Moray, who had inherited the title on the death of his predecessor less than a year before at Dupplin Muir. Moray advanced on his enemy and engaged, but the loss of order during the approach and the continuing archery on the flanks of the formation proved too much for the Scots and they soon began to withdraw. The centre division under the command of Robert the Steward advanced to engage Edward III's own command and the remaining Scottish formation under Douglas attacked the English right flank division, but to no useful purpose. Repulsed in all three fights, the Scots started to retire but were soon driven into one great mob of routing soldiers intent on putting as much distance between the enemy and themselves as quickly as possible. The pursuit of the Scots was relentless but brief. Edward recalled his men-at-arms, who had recovered their horses and joined the chase.

The scale of the victory was remarkable. Five Scottish earls had been killed in the action and so many knights and barons that the chronicler Fordoun abandoned any attempt to name them. The leadership of the Bruce party had been decimated in the battle, but Edward could be a vengeful man. Perhaps he felt the need to revenge himself on the Scots for his humiliation of 1327, but his victory was so complete and his casualties so light that it is difficult to understand why he felt it necessary or desirable to have the prisoners murdered. All the same, according to the English Meaux chronicle he had more than 100 of them beheaded on the day after the battle.

For the second time an emphatic victory in battle had presented Edward Balliol with the opportunity to realise his regal ambition. Appointments to government

15. The view from Halidon Hill, (*top*) to the west, (*middle*) south-east to the River Tweed, and (*bottom*) towards the north. The English position was virtually impregnable.

offices were made, supporters were given new grants of land and old grants were confirmed in an attempt to build a Balliol administration.

The supporters of the Balliol monarchy were not all members of the Disinherited. Edward Balliol had secured the support of various English magnates by offering them estates in Scotland in exchange for military service, the most prominent of these being Henry Percy. Percy had lost lands in Scotland during the first war of independence, but unlike the Disinherited he had his Scottish estates restored to him by Robert I. He chose not to be involved in the attempted Balliol restoration of 1332, but when Edward III declared his support for the Disinherited by joining Balliol at the siege of Berwick, Percy had become a retainer of Edward Balliol. The armed support of Percy was not given out of kindly generosity; the new king settled 2000 'marcates' (lands worth 2000 marks per year) of land south of the River Forth on his new ally. The estates given to Percy and the even larger territory – 2000 librates – ceded to Edward III meant that there would be very little of southern and central Scotland south of the Forth left in the hands of the new king.

If the outcome of battle could be so decisive, how did the Bruce cause survive at all, let alone recover and eventually triumph? The two great clashes of the early part

16. The counties promised to Edward III by Edward Balliol.

of the war were striking victories, but an army cannot maintain its morale indefinitely on the strength of past triumphs if the overall pattern of the war is not in their favour. The battlefield successes of the Bruce party may have been in smaller affairs, but they were also more numerous. The lesson presumably learned from each of the major battles of the preceding forty years was surely that tactical success in large general engagements was not the key to winning wars, as demonstrated by the battles of Falkirk and Bannockburn.

The success of Edward Balliol's first campaign in Scotland had been short-lived in the extreme. His resounding victory at Dupplin Muir had thrown the Scots into disarray, but their recovery was brisk. His hurried departure for the safety of Carlisle after the fight at Annan might be seen as a consequence of over-confidence, but his general position was not strong. Although he had been able to secure the attendance of several bishops at his Parliament the representation of lay landowners was very meagre. The only magnates to attend other than members of the Disinherited were the Earl of Fife, whose enthusiasm seems to have been largely dependent on the presence of Edward Balliol's forces, and Patrick, Earl of Dunbar, at this time a paid officer of Edward III.

The regularity with which certain Scottish nobles could change allegiance has made them the object of a great deal of criticism from Scottish medievalists, but the realities of fourteenth century politics meant that they had difficult paths to follow. At the height of his first attempt to achieve kingship, Edward Balliol had received the homage of Alexander Bruce, natural son of Edward Bruce and Earl of Carrick, only to lose it when he was overwhelmed at Annan. This renewed the pattern from a generation before, the apparently easy changes of allegiance enacted when the course of the war altered, but it is important to recognise that the chief responsibility of a baron was to pass on the family inheritance intact if not improved. In order to keep the head attached to the body or the lands attached to the landlord, any sensible person might feel the need to change sides on account of the fear that affects 'even the steadfast'. This was not a phenomenon limited to the Scottish nobility and gentry. The power of the Scots in northern England during the later stages of the previous wars had persuaded many Northumbrian and Cumbrian knights to accept the lordship of Robert I, but they all returned to Plantagenet allegiance with the end of hostilities in 1328. The fact that they were not heavily penalised for their desertion of their king would indicate that their plight in the face of overwhelming Scottish force was perfectly understood.

To what extent such changes of heart could be trusted was open to question. When David de Strathbogie was captured and then appointed as Guardian north of the Tay for David II in 1334, did John Randolph and his associates seriously believe that this was seen as a permanent transfer of loyalties? Strathbogie was one of Edward Balliol's most important lieutenants and was one of the men with a great deal to gain from the restoration of the Balliol monarchy. Perhaps his appointment implies that at a particular juncture Moray considered the value of Strathbogie as an instrument of the government in administering law and order greater than the threat of Strathbogie returning to the allegiance of Edward Balliol. If so, it speaks volumes for Moray's confidence that he could deal adequately with Strathbogie at some later date should it become necessary. Equally it may be that Moray feared the resentment that might be engendered by Strathbogie's execution, both in terms of offending localised sympathies and increasing the possibility of reprisals against Bruce supporters in the north-east.

Robert the Steward was another whose change of allegiance may not have enjoyed the complete confidence of his new king, Edward Balliol. Robert's lands were not greatly at risk to the claims of the Disinherited, so he could afford a realignment of his loyalties in a way that Douglas or Randolph could not. On the other hand, if David II were to die without a male heir, the crown would pass to Robert under the 'entail' – the order of succession confirmed by Parliament in 1318. His return to the Bruce party probably surprised no one.

The greatest concentration of baronial support for the Bruce cause was north of the Tay. When Robert I destroyed the Comyn family's control of north-east Scotland during his campaigns of 1308, he replaced them with men on whose loyalty he could depend, through proven allegiance and service or through the bonds of landholding and matrimony.

King Robert's policy of binding the great landholders to his lordship by the judicious use of landgrants and the marriages of his female relations to leading nobles effectively embedded the Bruce cause into the fabric of Scottish society. Many of the great lords owed the position of their family to their attachment to the Bruce party. If they were to retain the gains made they would have to support the Bruce party because satisfying the claims of the Disinherited would mean, for many of them, the loss of estates gained in the reign of King Robert. Even if they felt that their own holdings were free from the aspirations of the Disinherited there was the question of whether they wanted to be simply barons or barons in the close confidence of the King? This would prove to be the fatal obstruction to Edward Balliol's ambition. Too large a proportion of the nobility was attached to the Bruces. The Douglases and the Randolphs for example could not realistically be brought into Edward Balliol's allegiance unless they were willing to forego extensive lands, which at one time had belonged to Strathbogie and Beaumont's forebears.

The enormous resources of the Randolphs were generally beyond the range of Edward Balliol's operations other than the efforts of Strathbogie and Beaumont to establish their authority. A major raid by the two Edwards could penetrate as far as Elgin but a powerful force could not be maintained there indefinitely. As long as he could not permanently disable the Bruce party in the north, Edward's security would be in question. Not only could they operate from a relatively secure hinterland where they could offer stability and protection, but their tenants and neighbours could identify military service south of the Tay with not having the war conducted on their own doorsteps north of the Tay.

Despite the efforts of Strathbogie and Beaumont, the Bruce party was able to continue some form of administration. However rudimentary and vulnerable, they could more credibly claim to be the Scottish 'government' than Edward Balliol's party. Edward III's chamberlain at Berwick refused to account for the issues of the area of his responsibility other than Berwickshire and Roxburgh because the rest of Edward's domain in Scotland was beyond his control. The Bruce policy of resisting the ambitions of Beaumont and Strathbogie militarily and preventing them from forming a Balliol province in the north denied Edward the services of two of his more able lieutenants, whose abilities and armed strength could have helped stabilise his position in the south.

The absence of a consistent focus of government in the shape of a strong king or guardian allowed local potentates to further their ambitions. The 'good services' past and promised that John, Lord of the Isles offered to Edward Balliol never amounted to very much in the way of positive aid, but it cost Edward title to estates across the west of Scotland. John's effective neutrality was at least as useful to the Bruce party as it was to Edward. The Bruce hinterland in the north of Scotland was vulnerable to John's eastward expansion, and a vigorously conducted war in the north-east might well brought about the end of the Bruce cause and further territorial acquisitions to add to the MacDonald hegemony on the western seaboard. John's failure to pursue such campaigns suggests a lack of confidence in the ability of the two Edwards to defeat the Bruce party. If the Bruce cause were to triumph despite his active opposition John might have to face them in isolation. When John defected to David Bruce the price of his change of heart was his retention of the former crown estates in Skye and the return of the other estates to the crown.

The similarities to the earlier wars of independence tend to obscure the differences. The war of the 1330s was more 'chivalric' in nature. The need to perform valiant deeds and build a reputation as a flower of chivalry was an important aspect of life in the armigerous classes, as was the requirement to carry out acts of knightly courtesy. The growth of chivalry made the war in a sense more professional, easing the ransom and exchange of prisoners, but there were drawbacks. For instance, the Earl of Moray was captured whilst escorting a paroled enemy (the count of Namur) to the English army.

The nature of military operations by the Bruce party had changed since Robert I's reign. During that war, castles might be taken by subterfuge or surprise assault, but mostly they had to be starved out or they negotiated conditional surrender agreements like Dundee or Stirling. In this war the Bruce party gained access to the means of conducting close sieges in the formal style and acquired the technology to batter castles into submission. Obviously this had a very positive effect on the morale of Bruce party troops, but the effect on Balliol garrisons would have been at least as important. In the 1310s, a strong castle might hold out long enough to be relieved or obtain favourable capitulation terms from the besiegers. In the 1330s, Bothwell castle, one of the strongest in the country, only lasted three weeks in the face of 'boustour', a weapon fielded by the Bruce army. The future of isolated garrisons was not promising. With the Bruce forces greater exploitation of low-level ambush and patrol warfare, was typical of the everyday conduct of war in fourteenth-century Scotland, garrisons could easily lose control of their immediate surroundings. They then became a costly liability to the Balliol cause rather than an asset that collected taxes, raised troops and generally carried out the business of government. Each town or castle taken by the Bruce party enhanced the reputations of their leaders as paladins and encouraged the identification of the Bruce cause with the 'national' interest. Inevitably, the loss of these towns had a concomitant effect on the public perception of the Balliol cause.

The war at sea followed a similar pattern. Since as many as three dozen vessels might leave from one Scottish port, Aberdeen, in the course of a year in the 1320s and 1330s maritime trade was evidently an important concern. The vulnerability of shipping and the attractions of taking prizes encouraged Scottish and foreign ship owners to arm their vessels for protection and piracy. No doubt this was a crucial part of the development of piracy, for which the Scots would become, probably quite reasonably, infamous in the fourteenth century. The threat of French and Scottish commerce raiders and landing parties in the channel was another drain on the resources of Edward III. However, although the sea war favoured the Bruce party most of the time, and was vitally important to both English and Scottish interests there was no attempt by either side to concentrate a fleet and force a major battle. Edward III potentially had an enormous fleet available which the Bruce party could not hope to match. However, he could not afford to pay for a large patrolling fleet to dominate both the Irish and North Sea while maintaining a strong force of ships in the channel against coastal raids from France.

Sympathy for the Bruce position and admiration for Robert I as a genuinely heroic figure may not have been universal in Scottish society, but there was undoubtedly a good deal of both to be exploited by his son's supporters. The Balliol cause looked for, and to some extent found, popular support in their ancestral estates in Galloway, but in the thirty years and more since the deposition

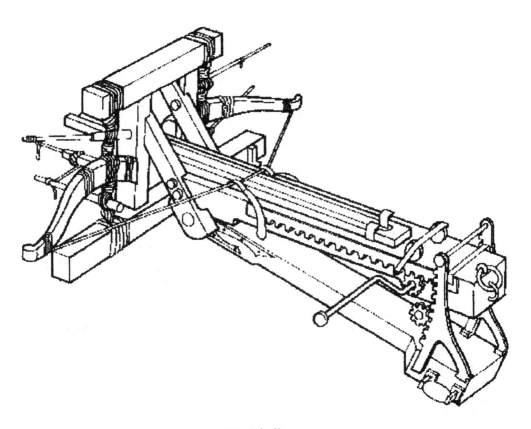

17. A ballista.

18. A catapult, a permanent exhibit at Caerlaverock Castle.

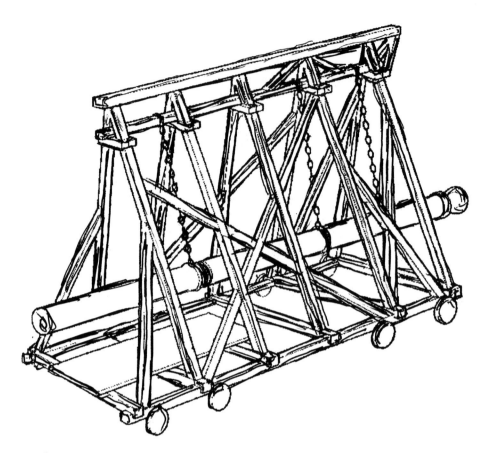

19. A battering ram. Rams such as this would normally be roofed to protect the crew
from the missiles of the defenders

of John I, the tradition of Balliol support must have worn thin and competition
for local dominance between the Maxwells and the MacDougals divided such
support as might have been available.

Edward Balliol may not have been identified as being particularly English, but
the Bruce party could certainly be identified as being profoundly Scottish. The
lengthy tradition of fighting the English that had developed since the invasion of
Edward I in 1296 probably did the Bruce faction no harm, but it can hardly have
done Edward Balliol any good. The Bruce party had a more simplistic and
accessible political position. The Balliol party was fighting for a relatively complex
political solution involving not only a change of dynasty and the restitution of
ancestral estates, but also the settlement of a large portion of southern Scotland on
Edward III and the acceptance of the feudal superiority of the king of England
over the king of Scots. The Bruce party could claim to be fighting for the rights
of the son of Scotland's hero king and the preservation of the traditional laws and
customs of the land.

Opposition to the Balliol cause was not the same thing as support for the Bruces. As
in the previous conflict some people chose to have no open commitment to either side,

claiming that they owed allegiance only to 'The Lion', meaning the heraldic device of the king of Scots, but in this context the term refers to the essentially abstract concept of the 'nation', that is to say Scotland as an institution rather than simply a dynastic possession. A declaration for the lion could be construed in a number of ways; as a means of denying personal allegiance to either side or to both, or it could represent a simple option in circumstances where an individual might have real doubts about who was the 'correct' regal candidate. King Robert's acquisition of the crown could hardly be described as normal constitutional practice, whereas King John had been chosen by a lengthy formal procedure, the authority of which had been accepted by all the candidates. Those adopting the lion as their cause may not have favoured the Bruces, but they did not favour the Balliols either. The success of the Bruce party in encouraging the identification of the national interest with the Bruce interest meant that any action taken by the 'lion' supporters was more likely to be advantageous to them than to the Balliols. The choice of symbol surely indicates their general sympathies and a hostile attitude to anything looking remotely like an occupation.

The level of support provided by Edward III would have been very visible. Although the combined strength of the garrisons was very small indeed this visibility would have been part of their function; to overawe opposition and generally 'show the flag' in the interests of Edward Balliol's kingship and Edward III's lordship in the ceded counties. Armies of any kind were not welcome visitors, the depredations of Balliol/Plantagenet garrisons caused major damage to the status of Edward Balliol, driving his active supporters to seek lordship elsewhere, so the uncommitted and disinterested could hardly be expected to join his cause. Even if they took no action at all other than to deny their area to the Balliol administration, that would aid the Bruce cause. Balliol military preparations would have to take account of these people for fear that they might become more active or that they could mask Bruce infiltration.

The difficulties of Edward Balliol were of course bonuses for the Bruce party. Although the power of Edward III was vital to the continuance of his struggle, let alone its successful conclusion, Edward Balliol was consistently undermined by his patron's actions and problems. Edward III's willingness to sanction the exchanges and ransoms which were an integral part of the chivalric code allowed the Bruce party to recover Moray and largely removed the spectre of long imprisonment during which the captured baron could not see to the security of his estate. Forbidding ransoms would have been a serious disincentive to soldiering in Scotland. The risks of service were considerable and the conditions uncomfortable, but the ransom of a wealthy man could compensate for that.

Edward III's increasing preoccupation with affairs in France and the difficulty of persuading troops to serve in Scotland reduced the capacity of Edward Balliol and Edward III's lieutenants to conduct effective operations other than sporadically. The willingness of the two Edwards to negotiate with the Bruce party and to offer or accept truces is not an indication that they felt confident of their position.

The real value of a major battlefield victory must have become all too apparent to the Balliol party after Halidon Hill. Despite the magnitude of the English victory and the wholesale surrender of castles and towns, the Bruce party was conducting operations against them in a matter of months. Within a year they were campaigning in the recently ceded counties. They were assisted in their resistance not only by the weakness of Edward Balliol, whose slender military resources were spread very thinly on account of the need for his supporters – both the Disinherited and the more recently acquired allies like Henry Percy – to secure the territory that they claimed from the enemy and also by the policy of Edward III himself. Possibly in an attempt to make the occupation unobtrusive, Edward had installed very small garrisons – tens rather than hundreds – in the castles that had fallen to his forces. This may have been politically desirable and perhaps unavoidable for financial reasons, but it was almost an invitation for the Scots to resume the fight. The garrisons provided an identifiable intrusion but did not have the power to discourage resistance.

The Bruce cause had not been wholly abandoned at any time. The Scots were reduced to holding only a handful of strongholds after the disaster at Halidon Hill, but this does not necessarily give the full picture. It had been the policy of Robert I to destroy castles that his forces captured to prevent them becoming bases for English troops in future wars, so it is possible that there were few castles in a defensible condition. Edward Balliol may have been able to call himself king, but for several months after his restoration he seems to have been unable to extend his rule effectively and the Scots were allowed a brief respite to reorganise.

The handful of castles in Scottish hands, scattered as they were, provided a framework for resistance, but it is unrealistic to see them as the sole strength of the Bruce party. Despite the stunning victory at Halidon the Balliol/Plantagenet forces were not able to extend their rule throughout Scotland, but were largely limited to the south and east of the country. The Scots could not oppose strong field forces which could penetrate into the less accessible areas of northern Scotland but equally the Balliol/Plantagenet forces could not establish dominance in areas where they could not be re-supplied from England other than for brief forays. Edward III was willing to embark on these operations in order to divert Scottish resistance from the southern counties that had been ceded by Edward Balliol, but he was unwilling to become bogged down in an endless series of campaigns in the north. If he could secure the castles and communities of the south, he could afford to leave the permanent conquest of the north to Edward Balliol and his associates. If they were successful Edward would have control of Scotland beyond the Forth because Edward Balliol was his vassal; if they failed he might reasonably hope to retain the southern counties as a buffer zone which would contain the Scots. At the very least he could reasonably hope that any Scottish warfare would be outside his own borders; an important consideration if he was going to press his claims in France through military intervention.

Edward's Scottish operations had real significance beyond the British Isles. He was eager to exploit any opportunity that might arise in Scotland, but his real ambitions lay in France. Edward had a claim to the throne of France through his mother Isabella, one much more realistic in legal terms than any claims to feudal suzerainty over Scotland. However the Scoto-French co-operation against English expansionism that had existed since the treaty of Paris in 1295 meant that he could not afford to make war in France without removing the risks of Scottish intervention on his own northern border. Despite enormous expenditure, Edward I had failed to conquer the Scots, and his campaigns in Flanders and France had been compromised by the demands of the Scottish front.

Edward III was prepared to forgo the acquisition of Scotland in its entirety and provide support for Edward Balliol to enjoy greater freedom of action elsewhere.

The cession of the southern counties of Scotland by Edward Balliol had not perhaps been as straightforward as Edward III had hoped. Instead of the wholesale transfer of Berwickshire, Selkirkshire, Dumfriesshire, Roxburghshire, Peebleshire and the Lothians that he had anticipated, Edward Balliol was determined to stick to the letter of their agreement and appointed commissioners to clearly measure out the 2000 librates. Nonetheless, by the summer of 1334 he had formed the basis of an administration for his new possessions and felt sufficiently secure to leave the completion of his Scottish operations to his lieutenants.

This was perhaps somewhat premature. Scottish towns might be in the hands of Edward III's forces or in the hands of his client Edward Balliol, but the war was not yet won. Almost before his back was turned the Scots had started to undermine his position. Robert the Steward – heir apparent to the young David II – raised a force to recover his lands in the Cowal peninsula. His successful attack on Dunoon castle inspired his tenants on the isle of Bute, who rose against the forces of David de Strathbogie and captured Rothesay castle. Within a matter of weeks the majority of the south-west (apart from Galloway where the Balliol cause enjoyed traditional loyalties) was in the hands of the Scots. Not all of the south-west had been ceded to the English, but had remained part of the realm of Edward Balliol. Balliol was unable to regain his position, but, more alarmingly for his patron, the Scots started to make inroads into the ceded counties so quickly that Edward III's chamberlain for Scotland was unable to collect the 'issues' – taxes, customs and rents – that Edward needed to pay for his Scottish garrisons.

Spring and summer 1334 saw a steady improvement in the fortunes of the Bruce party. Moray and the Stewart had been able to establish themselves as joint guardians; Richard Talbot, claimant to former Comyn family estates, had been defeated and captured in a small action near Linlithgow and the Disinherited had fallen out among themselves over a question of inheritance which led to the defection of Alexander Mowbray, a prominent Balliol supporter. The enforced defection of David de Strathbogie and the loss of Beaumont's castle at Dundarg before the end of September demolished the Balliol cause in the north and north-east.

The investment that Edward III had already made in Scotland was immense; unless Edward was prepared to write off his own interests in Scotland and those of the Balliol party he was going to have to mount another campaign. This could not be done overnight, and it was not until November 1334 that he was ready to take the field. Recruiting had not been an unqualified success. The royal household and the magnate retinues, combined with the levy troops of (primarily) the north of England and Wales, probably did not far exceed 4000 combatants. Of these rather more than 1000 were knights and men–at–arms and another 1500 or so were hobelars and mounted archers. A party of approximately 200 masons and labourers was recruited to form an engineering department which seems to have spent its time rebuilding Roxburgh castle which appears to be the only tangible achievement of the entire campaign.

Edward seems to have been dissatisfied with the turn out judging by his repeated demands for manpower, but this was still a very powerful force, particularly for a

20. Castle walls were topped with gantries like this to provide shooting positions.

winter campaign. The logistical effort involved in keeping the army fed was enormous yet supply of materiel was not the only problem to be overcome. Most of the men were obliged to serve for only forty days, and Edward was making fresh demands for men to replace them as early as the middle of December in order to maintain his ration strength. The appeals for fresh troops were less than effective. Despite his best efforts, Edward's army dwindled as men completed their service and went home. He had to disband his army before the end of February with very little to show for all his trouble except a host of massive debts.

The army itself was probably the cause of another blow to Edward's fortunes. The Earl of March had aligned himself with the Balliol party and had become a paid retainer of Edward III. He had modernised his castle at Dunbar and consolidated his control of the area under Edward III's kingship yet now reverted to the Bruce cause. He claimed that he could not protect himself against the Scots if he remained in Edward's service, but probably also because he could not protect his tenants – supposedly allies of the English/Balliol cause – from the indiscriminate foraging of the English army. If he could not provide good lordship to his tenants and allies he would not be able to maintain his authority among them.

The Balliol party was under pressure from the Scots, but Edward could not raise sufficient strength to risk a campaign north of the River Forth. This was particularly unfortunate for Beaumont. Although he had not been able to fully realise his claim for the earldom of Buchan, he had made some progress. However, by the winter of 1334 he was conducting the defence of the castle of Dundarg and was in desperate need of relief and the castle fell to the Scots sometime around Christmas – a serious blow to the fortunes of the Disinherited. Without Dundarg there was little chance of building a local administration strong enough to displace the Bruce party.

Beaumont had surrendered on terms, and Edward III made a large contribution to his ransom so that he could continue the struggle, but the loss of a first rate castle to the Scots was a doubly severe blow because of the nature of its capture. In the first War of Independence the Scots had never been able to acquire effective siege artillery and had to rely on starving garrisons out or on capture through subterfuge. Either of these approaches might easily require a lengthy close siege and therefore the garrison might realistically hope to be relieved by a field army or a sortie from a neighbouring garrison. Dundarg fell precisely because the Scots had acquired effective siege equipment and could now batter down a castle. If Dundarg was not safe, nor was anywhere else.

Beaumont joined Edward at Berwick after a very brief captivity, but the army that the English king had hoped would cow the Scots into submission had virtually disappeared. The completion of the magnates' contracts, desertion and the inability of Edward's administrators to provide sufficient troops and supplies to maintain his army at a viable size to prosecute the war adequately all took their toll. A prolonged campaign with no tangible results reflected badly on the king's authority and political and diplomatic concerns forced Edward to return to London to get on with the normal business of government.

Edward left Berwick in early February 1335 but did not abandon his Scottish establishment entirely. Indentures were made with various magnates to provide and command garrisons in those areas where he hoped to build an English pale, but the heavy cost of keeping large bodies of men under arms for any length of time precluded an aggressive occupation that could further his ambitions north of the border. The forces he could afford to commit were small, but he could depend on them to keep the Scots occupied while he made plans for this next expedition and to provide some support to the Balliol party.

The garrisons that Edward III left in place and the fleet he committed to the blockade of Scottish ports were never going to amount to anything more than a holding operation. Edward had come to the conclusion that his client, Edward Balliol would never be able to wrest control of Scotland north of the Forth and Clyde without the aid of a major campaign that would carry the conflict into the Bruce heartland of the north. Strathbogie was still active in the Atholl area but his position was increasingly vulnerable. Unless the power of Moray and the other Bruce magnates could be thoroughly broken, they would eventually be able to remove all that remained of Balliol influence from the north and be in a position to make inroads into the ceded counties and the estates of Balliol supporters in the south.

If Edward failed to prosecute the war vigorously, all the vast effort and expense of his campaigns to date would have been wasted. Defeat in Scotland had been instrumental in bringing about the downfall of Edward II, and his son was not prepared to run the same risk. His plans for an English pale south of the Forth were more realistic than his father's commitment to the complete conquest that Edward I had envisaged. But his attempt to bring Scots into his peace had been heavy-handed and his actions had alienated the very people he needed to enlist if he was to secure the ceded counties through a political settlement.

4

INCREASING THE PRESSURE

The winter campaign of 1334/35 fizzled out and Edward had little or nothing to show for the enormous sums he had laid out, not only for his own forces and in the repair of castles, but also for the army of Edward Balliol. Edward had been able to avoid paying the full wage rates for some of the troops because lords with Scottish ambitions had supplied them. A lord who hoped to become a Scottish magnate in the realm of Edward Balliol, assuming that Balliol was able to make himself *de facto* king of Scots, could not reasonably expect the king of England to shoulder all of the financial burden. On the other hand any of these lords was unlikely to be able to afford to keep troops in the field for any length of time without royal subsidy. Each of Edward's campaigns against the Scots – Weardale in 1327, Halidon in 1333 and the winter operations of 1334/5 had been a costly failure insofar as none of them had resulted in the comprehensive destruction of the Bruce party or even established a credible and sustainable administration in the lands ceded by Edward Balliol. Edward III's parliaments were less than forthcoming in authorising taxation to fund the Scottish war, so Edward was having to foot the bill from his own pocket and was accruing enormous personal debts.

The picture was not altogether bleak however. The Scots, under the leadership of Sir Andrew Moray, had been unable to eject all the garrisons that Edward III and Edward Balliol had put in place after Halidon. Some of these garrisons were isolated, and probably none of them could really be said to be effectively fulfilling their function of securing their localities for the two Edwards, but they were still a thorn in the flesh of the Scots and could provide a network of bases for raiding operations or a future invasion.

Through the diplomatic efforts of the French a truce had been made to run from February to midsummer 1335. Edward had refused to negotiate directly with the Scots because that would have extended a degree of diplomatic recognition to the

21. A trebuchet, after Payne-Gallway.

Bruce cause so the discussions were conducted with the assistance of French intermediaries though Edward had in fact already met informally with Scottish representatives at least once. During the early stages of the conflict he had received representatives from the Bruce party, but that had been to demonstrate to Edward Balliol that he could not be trifled with. If Balliol did not toe the line Edward III would be quite prepared to abandon him and either come to terms with the Bruce party or to continue the war on his own behalf with the intention of conquering Scotland outright.

The spring truce of 1335 suited the Scots and the two Edwards. It gave the Bruce and the Balliol parties a breathing space to conduct government, consolidate their positions and endeavour to gather political support in the community. For Edward III it was an opportunity to attend to domestic and diplomatic affairs and to plan for a new phase of the war. None of the parties would have assumed that the truce could be converted into a firm peace simply because there was really no room for a compromise. The policy of relatively limited military involvement had failed and Edward decided that if he was going to be able to recoup his losses he would have to mount a full-scale war with the objective of destroying the Bruce party through force of arms as opposed to imposing a political settlement

In May 1335, probably as a reaction to Edward III's preparations for the offensive that he was obviously going to mount at the conclusion of the truce, the Scots had sent David II and his queen – Joanna, the sister of Edward III – to Chateau Gaillard in France where they would be the guests of King Phillip for seven years. This was an encouraging development inasmuch as it indicated that the Scots were not totally confident of being able to protect their king. Admittedly it made the capture of David virtually impossible, but, on the other hand, French hospitality for an exiled King of Scots might be eroded if his cause was utterly destroyed. Indeed, Edward might be able to secure the person of the Scottish king as a bargaining counter in Anglo–French negotiations if he could gain an ascendancy in the French war that he was already contemplating.

Edward had raised an army of about 4000 for his last campaign, believing that this would be quite enough to deal with the scale of forces that the Scots would be able to mobilise in the winter months. He had come to accept that summer campaigns against an enemy that would not face him in the field was never going to bring his Scottish war to a favourable conclusion, and that the continual drain on his resources must sooner or later become a bone of contention at home if there were no victories to show for his efforts. Raising armies was all very well, but what was the point if they could not come to grips with the enemy and if their gains in one season were lost in the next? Edward decided to carry the war into the north of Scotland with the aim of crippling the Bruce party in the area of their greatest strength.

The new offensive called for a much greater commitment of manpower and money. For the earlier operations Edward had relied on the troops that could be supplied by magnates serving under contract and the levies of northern England. The army for the campaign of 1335 was drawn from the whole of England and also from Ireland and Wales, and further supplemented by allies on the continent such as the count of Juliers, who served in person with a force of men-at-arms.

Most of the army mustered at Berwick by 23 June where it was divided into two parts. One division set out for Carlisle under Edward III where it was joined by the force of Henry Beaumont, the remainder was placed under the command of Edward Balliol. Their intention was to traverse southern Scotland and effect a union of the two forces in the region of the river Clyde before moving north in great strength in the hopes of bringing the Scots to battle and finally destroying the Bruce party forces before they could consolidate the gains they had made in the preceding months.

Well aware that they could not face the enemy in battle with any hope of success, the Scots had adopted the scorched earth tactics that Robert I had pioneered in the first War of Independence. The two English forces had complete freedom of movement, but there was very little to be found by foraging parties. Neither force encountered any noticeable resistance in the southern counties until Balliol's command reached Cumbernauld. A peel belonging to David de Strathbogie, who at this time was still in the Bruce party following his capture by Moray in Lochaber in September 1334, held out briefly, but was forced to surrender when the besiegers managed to set the main building on fire.

By the middle of July the two Edwards had concentrated their forces and established themselves just north of the Forth at Airth. The campaign had not been a runaway success. The Scottish Guardian, the Earl of Moray, was conducting operations in their rear and was causing problems to their logistics effort, but they could not bring him to battle. A hungry army is seldom a happy or confident army and Edward was faced with the prospect of having to yet again disband a hugely expensive force without it having achieved anything more than devastating raid through lowland Scotland. At this point he had a stroke of good fortune which came about through the defeat of one of his allies in an engagement in and around Edinburgh.

The count of Namur, Edward's brother-in-law, had arrived late for the muster of the army and had decided, despite advice to the contrary, to make his own way north to join the king. His force – a handful of knights and 100 or so men-at-arms had been supplemented by a party of English reinforcements consisting of a few knights and about 100 archers. This would appear to be quite a powerful following, but Namur was considered to have acted rashly by trying to travel through Scotland with such a small force under his command, which perhaps gives us some idea of the size of formations that conducted the majority of the fighting through most of the war. Despite harassment by the Scots under Moray and the Earl of March, Namur had almost reached Edinburgh when the Scots finally caught up with him at Burghmuir. A running fight ensued that continued through the town and Namur's force occupied the ruins of Edinburgh castle, where some of his men killed their horses in the breaches of the castle walls in an attempt to make a barrier.

With no prospect of relief, Namur was forced to surrender. His company had suffered heavy casualties, including one female soldier who had killed her assailant, Richard Shaw, in the same moment as her assailant killed her. The gender of this 'woman-at-arms' was only discovered when the bodies were being stripped of their armour at the end of the engagement. The chronicler Bower seems to have been at least as impressed by the rarity of two mounted soldiers simultaneously transfixing one another with their lances as with the fact that one of them was a woman. The level of personal skill required for a person to be able to fight on horseback at all is very considerable and combat with a couched lance was perhaps the most challenging aspect of mounted warfare. For a woman to be accepted into an intensely 'chivalry-conscious' and male-orientated group such as the Count of Namur's company means she must surely have been something of a paragon of knightly virtue.

Namur surrendered to Moray, agreed a ransom of £4000, and gave his word that he would not bear arms against David II. This was all to the good as far as the Scots were concerned, but Moray, in order to show that despite their inability to face the English in large conventional battles the Scots nobility and gentry were as much committed to the ideals of chivalry as anyone else, chose to escort his honoured prisoner to the English and was duly captured himself. Edward III, realising that Moray was the most competent commander among the Scots refused to allow him to be ransomed. The Scots had to make do with less effective leadership for some time until the appointment of Sir Andrew Moray, a wealthy baron from the north-east.

The ransoming or exchange of prisoners was a well-established practice. The financial attractions for the captor and the avoidance of an indefinite captivity for the prisoner are self-evident, but there were drawbacks. The advantage gained through the capture of a prominent or competent leader could be lost almost as soon as it had been achieved as long as the captive could find the money to pay for his release. A ban on ransoming would have been a serious disincentive to army service, particularly for those English nobility and gentry who had no landed interest in Scotland, but whose military service was essential if Edward III's Scottish ambitions were to be made a reality. Army wages were good, particularly for lords, knights and men-at-arms, but not good enough to make the risks of serving in Scotland worthwhile if there was no chance of earning large sums through ransom, and certainly not good enough to make the possibility of years as a prisoner a worthwhile risk if there was no prospect of being liberated through payment or exchange.

The loss of Moray was a severe blow to the Scots. His defeat meant that the only noteworthy opposition to the power of Edward III in the south of Scotland was the Earl of March. Without a major improvement in the fortunes of the Bruce cause he could hardly be expected to resist indefinitely in his castle at Dunbar, but no move was made against him and he remained in Bruce service.

Edward III and Edward Balliol had made their way to Perth by the first week in August and the town had surrendered to them immediately. For the next five or six weeks Edward III stayed in the town while Edward Balliol led a force – about 800 strong according to the Bridlington Chronicle and probably predominantly men-at-arms and mounted archers since the majority of his force seems to have been taken from the retinues of English magnates. The great army that had been raised for the invasion could not be kept under arms for any longer, partly because of the strain on the English exchequer and partly because the troops' contracts were coming to an end. In any case, in the absence of Scottish military activity of any stature there was not really a great deal for them to do. The lands of Bruce sympathisers could be raided and their castles captured, but it was hardly necessary to have such a large army on hand to carry out such minor operations. Edward had hoped that a major demonstration of military power would bring at least some of the Scots to terms, and he was right.

David de Strathbogie, titular Earl of Atholl returned to the Balliol party, allegedly because the two Edwards were now willing to promise to uphold various aspects of Scottish legal and ecclesiastical independence. In practice both he and Balliol were simply accepting political reality. If the Bruce party was finished – and there was good reason to believe that it was – his own prospects were poor to say the least. He was after all a traitor to the Balliol cause. Admittedly, he had joined the Bruce party under duress, and his appointment as guardian in the north of Scotland for David II had probably been an attempt to put him so firmly in the Bruce camp that he would be unable to restore his position in the Balliol administration. On the other hand the Balliol cause could not afford to do without the services of David de Strathbogie. As one of the most powerful northern lords he was vital to the war effort.

The earls of Fife and Menteith joined the Balliol cause, but with Edward III's army on their doorstep they really had little choice in the matter. The fact that the Earl of Fife had already changed sides twice but was still accepted into the peace of Edward Balliol and confirmed in his estates indicates that Balliol was hopeful, if not confident, that his own position as king could be made acceptable to the political community. If he was going to rule without the presence of an English army to enforce his kingship Edward Balliol needed to gain the allegiance of magnates from the Bruce party, and he would not attract them if they felt that they would be disinherited. Men claiming to represent Robert the Steward took part in negotiations, but no guarantees were offered for his physical safety let alone his estates. The Steward does seem to have come to Edward's peace shortly afterwards, possibly because of a descent on his estates in the west of Scotland by troops from Ireland. The return of Strathbogie to his former allegiance offered the possibility of building a permanent pro-Balliol interest in the north of Scotland as a counter to the power of the Earl of Moray and his associates. His extensive lands would constitute a useful recruiting area and he had probably been able to consolidate and even extend his lordship as Earl of Atholl to some degree while he had been in the Bruce party.

Edward disbanded his army and headed south to arrange the administration of the eight counties that had been promised him in return for his support. He put in train the repair of the castles that would be the basis of the government in southern Scotland, particularly Edinburgh, which he hoped would replace Berwick as the tactical and strategic headquarters for any future operations in Scotland.

At last, the investment that Edward had made in Scotland in the interests of Edward Balliol and on his own behalf could be said to have begun to show results. Many of the freeholders and barons of the southern counties that had remained steadfast in the Bruce cause now saw no alternative to acceptance of the Plantagenet and Balliol government. Edward could appoint his own men to government office or ecclesiastical positions with some confidence that they would be able to carry out his policies unimpeded by the Bruce party. The issues of the ceded areas – taxes, customs and the profits of justice could be collected and disbursed to fund the administration and thereby reduce the demands that his Scottish wars were making on his over-stretched exchequer.

The financial burden of the Scottish campaigns was enormous. The wages bill for the operations of summer 1335 alone had been in the vicinity of £25,000 without taking account of sums made over to Edward Balliol to support his own, theoretically independent, army and household. In addition to these obvious costs Edward had been obliged to pay for extensive (and expensive) diplomatic missions to the French and papal courts. He also had to make contributions to the ransoms of several men who had been unlucky enough to be taken prisoner by the Scots (£400 for Henry Beaumont alone) and he had had to make provision for the administrators who had made the conduct of his affairs north of the border possible in the first place.

A full peace had not yet been formally secured, there were still elements of Scottish resistance. However, with so much of the Bruce leadership either in his peace or in his prisons Edward could realistically suppose that the war had been successfully concluded and that a permanent settlement confirming his possession of the ceded counties and the kingship of Edward Balliol under the feudal authority of Edward himself was in his grasp.

Had the effort been worthwhile? The ceded counties had suffered a great deal from the depredations of the armies of both sides and it might take some time before the rule of law could be established throughout his new possessions, yet they represented some of the best agricultural land in the British Isles. Though it might well be years before economic recovery was complete and until the trading towns returned to the prosperity that they had enjoyed in the past, there was no doubt that they could and would recover and in due course make a profitable contribution. The material benefits of extending his rule into southern Scotland were potentially enormous, but they were not the only consideration. If Edward could permanently establish his government there his prestige would be enhanced as a successful warrior king both at home and abroad and the disasters of his father's reign would be avenged. A firm peace in the north, made on his terms would give him greater freedom to pursue ambitions in other directions, namely France.

5
CONTINUAL WAR

If there is one aspect of life in the medieval period that is crucial to our understanding of the willingness of the Scots to continue the war in the face of repeated disasters it is the concept of 'good lordship'. If a landlord wished to maintain his position in the community he – or occasionally she – would have to secure and retain the goodwill of tenants and allies as well as keep on the right side of the king and local potentates. As we have seen, loyalty to the king was often dependent on the realities of living in a war zone. Loyalty to a magnate could supersede allegiance to the monarch. When a great lord like Patrick, Earl of March transferred his support from one king to another the majority of his tenants would be likely to follow suit because they might find themselves forfeited by their immediate feudal superior. They would in any case be likely to follow their lord's change of heart on the grounds that if a powerful noble felt that he could not resist pressure to change sides, how could a minor landowner avoid coming to the same conclusion?

A lord – particularly a magnate – was more than just a landlord. His more important tenants owed him rents and military service, but they were also involved in other aspects of their lord's relationship with the community. The tenants witnessed the lord's charters and sat on his courts; they were obliged to give him hospitality and advice in exchange for the lands they held from him. The tenants, then, gave a great deal to the lords, but it was not an entirely one-sided relationship. The tenant expected protection and counsel from his lord, particularly in times of crisis, and there were a great many crises in the Scottish society of the fourteenth century.

The tenant would hope that the burdens imposed on him would not be too onerous. He expected that his lord would be ready to stand up for his rights and interests but most importantly, he hoped that his lord would make leadership decisions that would not lead them both into dangerous situations in the fraught political and military struggles that comprise the Wars of Independence. When the pressure of events required a change of affiliation on the part of a great lord, the tenant hoped that the lord would be able to arrange the secure tenure of his followers. If the lord in question reverted to his previous allegiance his tenants hoped that he would be able to continue to protect their position. In most cases the superior would be able to procure the necessary safeguards for his tenant without much difficulty because the contending factions in the community would be more than happy to acquire their future support and of course to deny that support to the opposition.

A change of allegiance might be forced on an individual or community by the passage of an army and the establishment of a garrison in the area, but this could be counter productive. When the Earl of March abandoned the Balliol/Plantagenet party and returned to the Bruce cause he did so, at least in part, because he could not protect his tenants and adherents from the English garrisons in his area who were raiding the properties of Bruce and Balliol sympathisers indiscriminately. The Earl really had little choice if he was going to retain the respect of his people and maintain his authority among them.

Lordship was an important factor in motivating people to adopt one side or another, but it was not the only consideration. Many Scots supported the Balliol cause for legitimate reasons. The Balliol claim to the throne was better than the Bruce claim in terms of succession by primogeniture and the Bruce position was compromised by the murder of John Comyn in 1306. The obvious English support for Edward Balliol, whilst vital if his party was to be successful, was also counter-productive. As long as the Disinherited were clearly reliant on English forces the Bruce party would have an advantage in the propaganda war. Any castle held against the Bruce party could easily be portrayed as symbol of English occupation, even if the members of the garrison were largely, or even exclusively, Scots, which quite often they were. Apart from the issue of who should be king, there were very real attractions for Scots to enlist in the garrisons of Edward III and Edward Balliol. The prospect of regular wages would be a very positive incentive, but perhaps more importantly, especially for minor landowners, membership of the local garrison might help to protect their property from raids and requisitions. The other influence that we should bear in mind is that of the local community. If there were strong local feeling for the Balliol kingship it would be difficult for an individual to overtly support the Bruce party and vice versa.

There were many factors influencing the decision of which side to fight for, but that does not tell us who was actually going to do the fighting. In theory, most of the people who held land for army service were obliged to serve their superior for forty days a year. In addition to this they shared the obligation of all able-bodied subjects to serve the king for forty days in defence of the realm. In theory, then, a military tenant, holding land from one superior could be called out for eighty days unpaid service a year. This was a viable contribution to the armed strength of the country in the days of the brief wars of manoeuvre that had characterised the Anglo-Scottish wars of the twelfth century or the campaigns that Scottish kings had undertaken to consolidate their rule in the highlands and islands, but it was hardly adequate as a means of raising forces for the long haul of a war of national

22. Infantry in close order; vital agaisnt cavalry but disastrous against archers.

resistance to conquest. Those lords on both sides whose inheritances were at risk obviously had enough at stake to make it worthwhile to stay in the field for as long as it took, but maintaining a worthwhile force would have been a huge problem.

The burden of military service did not fall only on landowners. Every male member of the society had some level of obligation to serve at his own expense and with his own arms, but in practice the large quantities of weapons imported by the government would suggest that arms were in fact distributed by the government to those who could not provide their own equipment and this is supported by the capture of a large cache of pikes by Edward Balliol's troops after the battle of Dupplin Muir. A modest quantity of weapons might be the property of an landlord who intended to equip his own following or perhaps the stock of a merchant hoping to turn a profit out of the war, but such a large arsenal – apparently 4000 weapons – surely indicates an investment by the state. The demands of an agricultural economy meant that for most of the year the bulk of the people were needed on the land. Neither side could maintain large bodies of men for any length of time without adversely affecting agricultural productivity. This was probably more of a problem for the Balliol party than for the Bruce faction because the amount of territory that could be considered genuinely secure for the Balliol party was never very extensive.

If Edward Balliol was to be able to hold on to the territory that fell to his forces in the aftermath of Halidon Hill, let alone expand his sphere of influence at the expense of his enemies, he would have to hold a network of castles, fortresses and towns through which he could exercise his rule. To a considerable extent his chief

23. An arming cap, designed to be worn under a chainmail hood or helmet.

supporters could achieve this if they could secure their claims to Scottish lordships. If Beaumont could make good his claim to the Earldom of Buchan or Strathbogie his claim to Atholl they would have the power to replace tenants and freeholders in those areas with their own supporters. This would not only improve the recruiting potential of the Balliol cause in general, it would deprive the Bruce party of manpower and financial resources, it would damage the relative security of their administration north of the Forth and damage the credibility of David II's government. If his party could not protect their supporters in the north where there was a tradition of stable Bruce government dating back to before Bannockburn, how could they hope to extend their rule and provide 'good lordship' in the south where they had to combat a network of Balliol and Plantagenet garrisons? On the other hand, uprooting freeholders was hardly going to engender confidence in the community that the Balliol government would provide good lordship and displaced free tenants would have a powerful incentive to support the Bruce party vigorously.

Balliol, in order to develop his status as king, was therefore obliged to take the war to the enemy outside the eastern littoral for both military and political reasons. To rule Scotland he would have to displace the Bruce hierarchy in the north. This could only happen if the various disinherited lords had the opportunity to establish themselves in the lordships they aspired to, which inevitably meant that Edward Balliol was deprived of their military strength for as long as it took to overcome Bruce resistance in those localities. The dispersal of the Disinherited to their estates reduced the ability of Edward Balliol to react offensively to Bruce party operations and made him increasingly reliant on the manpower and money of Edward III, which in turn damaged his credibility as king. If his lieutenants were *not* allowed to pursue their claims the Bruce party would be able to consolidate their power base beyond the Forth; if they *were* encouraged to do so they must obviously take their troops with them, thus reducing the forces available to Edward Balliol for operations elsewhere.

Edward Balliol was beset by political difficulties as well as military ones. As we have seen, the price of Plantagenet support was the cession of the most of the south of Scotland. This was not a situation likely to commend his government to the Scottish political community; even his carefully selected parliament took a lot of persuasion to ratify his promises to Edward III, but he could not afford to renege on his agreement. When it seemed that he was dragging his feet Edward III issued safe-conducts to representatives of David II's government, implying that if Balliol did not toe the line Edward was prepared to consider a negotiated settlement that would leave the entire Balliol party out in the cold.

Even if Edward Balliol could retain the favour of Edward III there was a limit to the aid he could count on from England. The financial burden of supporting a client king in Scotland could not be borne indefinitely by Edward III's exchequer. Unless the Balliol party could bring their campaigns to a successful conclusion that would repay Edward's investment in Scotland they would sooner or later lose the English financial and military input that he needed to establish his kingship and the diplomatic support to get that kingship recognised abroad. Without that recognition his position as king would always be under threat from a pro-Bruce recovery sponsored by a foreign power. If Balliol could mount a *coup* against the Bruce government with the support of Edward III, David Bruce might well be able to mount a similar operation against the Balliol administration in the future.

As if he did not have enough problems, he had to be wary of his own supporters. Once it became apparent that Edward III was not prepared to commit his entire power to war in Scotland it became increasingly difficult to secure defections from the Bruce camp other than by main force, and if he was seen to be not winning the war the attractions of changing sides became rather stronger for his own supporters. If they could not win estates by fighting, they might be able to acquire some portion of them through negotiations with the Bruce government.

The temporary defection of one of his most important lieutenants – David de Strathbogie – had been secured at sword point and could be put aside as part of the fortunes of war, but the Disinherited were not absolutely united about who was entitled to inherit what. A land dispute concerning properties claimed as the inheritance of the Mowbray family could not be amicably settled and led to the defection of the Mowbrays to the Bruce party. This obviously weakened the Balliol party militarily because the Mowbrays immediately set about trying to recover their lands by force, but it damaged Edward Balliol's prestige as king because he could be seen to have failed to provide 'good lordship' to some of his closest associates. If he could not or would not protect the interests of his own comrades in arms there was little to attract people outside the Disinherited to his service. The whole affair reflected badly on his regal function as a source of justice and probably did nothing to enhance his status among the rest of his supporters. The disinherited were, in any case, a small group. Any reduction in their numbers would lead Edward Balliol towards ever-greater reliance on the men and money of Edward III. The more apparent his dependence on English arms, the more he would be identified as the agent of an English occupation and less as a king in his own right. To some extent of course Edward Balliol *was* the agent of Edward III, but he did have every intention of being an effective ruler over those parts of Scotland that he had not promised to Edward III. Unfortunately for him and his adherents the overwhelming majority of his domain had to be conquered if he was to rule and the resources available to him were slender.

The Bruce party had problems of their own. The campaigns of the Disinherited forced them to conduct operations all over the country and interfered with recruiting, movement of forces, the collection of taxes and the import of munitions. All of the more important trading towns were located on the eastern seaboard and almost all of them had fallen to Balliol and Plantagenet forces after Halidon Hill. A large proportion of the arms and armour of both sides was imported from the Low Countries, and the only serious cash-raising exports of the Scottish economy were wool and hides. The revenues of the Bruce government were seriously compromised by the loss of the more important wool-producing areas to the Balliol/Plantagenet administration. The loss of Berwick, Edinburgh, Perth and Dundee meant that the Scots had to rely on Aberdeen as their chief port, as they had in the first War of Independence. The significance of this was not lost on Edward III and the main focus of the war at sea was on commerce raiding to deny the Scots access to the markets of the Low Countries for the sale of wool and the purchase of arms.

24. A thoroughly well-equipped infantryman.

Leadership was another problem for the Scots. Edward Balliol was a man in the prime of life, but David II was a small boy. It is perfectly possible that people who preferred the Bruce cause, or for that matter those who really supported no cause at all, chose to give their allegiance to Edward Balliol for the sake of having a grown man govern the country in his own interest rather than have a noble govern in the name of a child-king. Even if the Bruce party had been completely united behind one leader throughout the war – and that was most certainly not the case – a regency government did automatically enjoy the same prestige as a regal administration. Any magnate appointed or elected Guardian was almost bound to be suspected of furthering his own interests while he held the reins of government. The diplomatic status of the Bruce party was less than secure. As long as it suited the interests of French kings, the Scots could look for, and generally receive, support for their efforts against the English. The beginning of the series of conflicts that we call the Hundred Years War was a cloud on the political horizon, but was not necessarily inevitable. If an Anglo-French war could be avoided by diplomatic means, the price of even a temporary peace for France might easily include the end of their alliance with the Scots. Any change in French policy would be likely to have serious repercussions for Scottish relations with the Pope. Although the Scottish clergy played a less prominent role in the Second War of Independence than it had in the first, its influence was still considerable. If papal pressure led them to whole-hearted support for Edward Balliol – or indeed for Edward III who had made it clear that he had not completely abandoned his own claims, however questionable, to Scottish suzerainty – the credibility of the Bruce cause would be undermined politically and, because of the immense landed wealth of the church, financially.

Both sides had to contend with specific obstructions to their policies but there were also problems that they shared. As in any civil war there was bound to be a significant part of the society that favoured neither side. Often these people could be cajoled into co-operation, but threats seldom produce willing allies. The passage of an armed force through a particular area might bring people into the 'peace' of Edward Balliol or Edward Plantagenet or David Bruce, but the reliability of such converts was unlikely to last any longer than the arrival of a force from the other side. As the war progressed depopulation became an issue. There was not much value in the acquisition of land if there were no people to tenant it. Deserted farms would yield neither troops nor taxes. Abandonment of the land through war exacerbated the fall in population that was by the close of the thirteenth century starting to be felt all over Europe and would become increasingly apparent with the arrival of the great plague epidemics of the 1340s.

There were also geographical considerations. Professor Barrow has convincingly demonstrated that lowland Scotland had as good a road network as most countries in fourteenth-century Europe, but that does not say a great deal. The roads were still few and far between and probably of just as poor a quality as would be found in France or England. Yet they were good enough to allow the inland garrisons of the Balliol and Plantagenet administrations to be replenished by wagon convoys and for siege equipment to be moved around the country. Inevitably this meant that such convoys were vulnerable to attack simply because they *were* confined to the roads and therefore the Scots could easily intercept them. The presence of a strong escort might deter an ambush party, but the troops for the escort would often, if not always, have to be drawn from the existing garrisons, thus diluting further what would usually have been very small forces in the first place. The roads, such as they were, did not always conform to the Roman pattern of 'shortest distance between two points' because of the distribution of viable fords and bridge sites. The route from one town to another might have to wind back and forth a good deal in order to form a practicable route; consequently journeys could take rather longer than we might expect, increasing the time that convoys were vulnerable.

The weather was a problem for everyone. The Scottish climate was a little warmer than it is today, but it was much wetter. If the roads were poor at the best of times they would have been even worse in the wet. Many river crossings were fords rather than bridges, and were therefore quite likely to be become impassable after a couple of days of rain. As far as possible bulk cargoes would be moved by sea, but the ships were small, slow and vulnerable to attack by privateers or pirates. English, Scottish, French and Flemish captains were attracted by the possibility of becoming suddenly rich at the expense of the combatant parties so traders banded together in convoys, accepting the delays incurred by having to wait for the convoy to gather and then having to travel at the speed of the slowest vessel.

The ships themselves were not built specifically as warships, but were merchant vessels with a larger than usual crew and might have temporary fighting platforms at the bow and stern for archers and spearmen. This practice raised the centre of gravity of the ships, making them top-heavy and difficult to manoeuvre. Navigation was as much an art as a science so skippers were inclined to hug the coastline as far as possible and the high incidence of beachings was due to the reduced seaworthiness of merchant ships converted for war.

The fighting crews of these ships differed little, if at all, from their counterparts on land. Obviously, a man in armour was almost certain to drown should he be unfortunate enough to fall into the water, but this does not seem to have dissuaded troops from wearing it. Presumably the benefits were considered to outweigh the disadvantages.

In general, historians tend to focus on the behaviour of armies. This is scarcely surprising, since the clash of armies is such a dramatic event and the mustering of armies usually generates a good deal of documentary record. This does make for a rather misleading view of the practice of war however because a general engagement on a grand scale or the movement of large forces are not really typical of the military experience of the fourteenth century. Although several campaigns involving large forces were conducted in Scotland and the north of England in the 1330s and 1340s, service in small garrisons or 'meinies' or 'ledings' (Scottish terms for 'retinues') was the more common experience. Whilst English forces and Scots in English service, whether in garrisons or in field armies, were recruited for wages, their opponents were generally serving to recover lands or to discharge their obligations as tenants or to perform the forty days 'common army' service that was the duty of all able bodied subjects.

Indeed, in 1319 Robert I had enacted legislation which clearly defined these responsibilities. A person with an annual income of £10 or more from rents or

£40 and over from goods was obliged, in theory anyway, to provide themselves, or a substitute, with sufficient kit to make them fit for service in the main line of battle. The aketon, bassinet, and steel-splinted gloves that they were obliged to acquire conform to the standards we might expect to find among the waged 'regular' infantry to be found in any other European army of the fourteenth century.

Interestingly, even surprisingly, there is no mention of a shield. In close combat a shield could be something of an encumbrance to a man trying to control a large spear, but the value of a shield against archery is obvious. The fact that shields are ignored perhaps suggests that the power of the longbow was not so apparent to fourteenth century soldiers as it seems to us, 700 years later. It is possible that a shield was so much an integral part of the kit of a fully armed soldier that it was not necessary to mention it, but this is surely unlikely given that the balance of the kit is carefully itemised in the legislation. At Neville's Cross the Scots had relied on their shields and armour to reduce casualties from archery. If the shield had not been an important factor in the military fashions of medieval Scotland, its widespread adoption by the 1340s may have been a response to the development of the longbow by commanders like Henry Beaumont in the 1330s.

These '£10 men' referred to in the 1319 Act of Parliament were obviously not the bulk of the population, but equally obviously they were a large enough segment of the society to be worthwhile targeting as a specific group. They must also have been a part of the community that could be easily identified as possessing that level of wealth and presumably, the kit required of them was at least believed to be within their financial capacities. The low-intensity localised warfare of the 1330s and 1340s was not however a conflict of mass armies, and it is probably fair

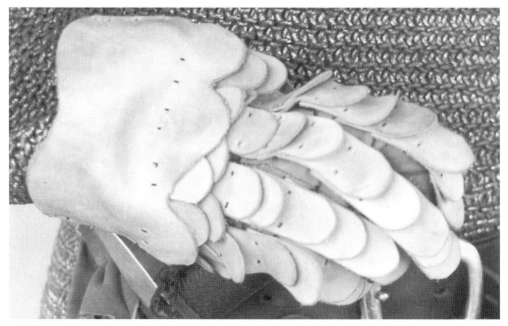

25. Unusual leather gauntlets.

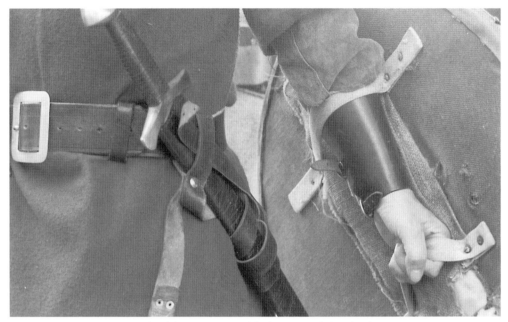

26. A shield, note its padded grip and the thickness.

to assume that the majority of the troops who served in the small formations that conducted most of the fighting for both sides would have fallen into the '£10' category of service. Militarily they were the people with the right kit for the job, but they were also the people who had interests worth protecting and with formal, individual obligations to their lords. If they did not serve they could expect to lose their free tenancy rights, and if their lands were occupied by someone else because of the shifting fortunes of war they were unlikely to regain possession unless they were willing to fight for it.

Lower down the social spectrum the burden of equipment was much lighter. A man with goods to the value of half a cow was obliged to have either a bow and two dozen arrows or a spear. While the latter category might have proved useful in times of national emergency, they were could hardly be described as being properly equipped for lengthy field service. When men like these were called out, it was surely to provide a large force from a relatively small area. The power to muster all able-bodied men lay with magnates, particularly earls. Responsibility for raising troops might extend to entire sherrifdoms, and was potentially subject to abuse by ambitious nobles who might demand the service due to the crown and deploy that service in their own interests. During his period as a Guardian, the future Robert I had to make a written affirmation that he would refrain from raising 'the army of Carrick', that is, the armed strength of the area, not just his own tenants for his own purposes. The Bishop and his neighbours were objecting to Bruce disrupting the community by conscripting their tenants for his wars. The 'common army' service was due from every member of the community, and could therefore produce a large force, but mostly unarmoured spearmen. It would be easy to dismiss the military value of the rank and file of the 'common army'.

27. A light infantryman with spear and staff sling.

Bruce, and no doubt others, abused their authority to enlist these troops and presumably thought it worthwhile to do so.

Establishing 'lordship' for the rival magnates of the Bruce and Balliol/Plantagenet camps was more than simply acquiring a particular estate, it was also a matter of securing administrative powers throughout a region. What role common army service played in the normal conduct of Anglo-Scottish wars is hard to identify. It was too plentiful a supply of manpower to be disregarded, but unarmoured, horseless spearmen would have limited value in the highly mobile raiding operations of the 1330s and 1340s. If, through a system of rotation, an earl could keep some of these men in service continually it might well have been worthwhile to provide the necessary mount and arms for the duration of a man's service. The battlefield drills of the fourteenth century did not have to be particularly intricate, so forty days of service performed two or three years running would almost inevitably bring about a certain level of competence. Those who owed military service for landholdings were not excused 'common army' service. Their obligation to serve their superior was a function of their 'rent'. If the superior was the king, a military tenant could theoretically be in continuous service for eighty days at a stretch. Not much of a problem perhaps for the holder of a money feif, but a long time for a landlord to be absent from his business.

On the eve of Bannockburn Robert I had dismissed under-equipped men from the main body of his army. The army that remained was hardly a 'corps d'elite', but they certainly constituted a well-armed and – because he took pains to ensure that they had been mustered some weeks before the battle – well trained and articulated force. The formations that fought in the period between Halidon Hill and Neville's cross would have conformed to that pattern. This does not mean that the men who served under the various Guardians who ruled the country on behalf of David II were all from the class of relatively wealthy farmers and town-dwellers that constituted the £10 or £40 men described in the legislation. Because the forces that were involved in the day-to-day conduct of the war were so tiny, more significant figures in the society would have been able to afford to supply their followers with equipment if need be and the spoil of the battlefield or from a surrendered stronghold would have been a useful source of equipment. The arms and armour of the defeated are traditionally part of the reward of the victor in most societies in any period of history. Lords and magnates with estates to defend or recover needed to have forces at their disposal, but they could not afford to maintain large bodies of men day in day out. It was much more practical to have a small, mobile force that could take on minor enemy units and outrun any serious opposition. It is important to bear in mind just how small the units were on either side. When Robert the Steward descended on the Balliol garrison of Dunoon in 1334 to recover his inheritance he lead an 'army' of 400, and that was a sizeable force engaged in a fairly major operation. The armies that fought at Halidon Hill were the product of concentrated recruiting on both sides, but it is doubtful if even the Scottish army – generally believed at the time to have been the larger of the two – was much more than 10,000 strong. Even the unusually large army amassed by Edward III for his offensive in the summer of 1335, a force that was calculated to impress the Scots through weight of numbers, only just surpassed 14,000 at its peak.

There were really two distinct types of army. The force assembled for national defence in Scotland or England was rather different from the force mustered for an offensive. An English defensive army, like the one gathered for the battle of Myton, was much more representative of the population than a force mustered for an invasion of Scotland. The latter was a contract army, embodied for a given duration and essentially comprising paid soldiers who had volunteered for service. Many of these would be experienced, trained men for whom army service was a normal part of life. The defensive army might have a number of such men in its ranks, but the bulk of the troops were simply discharging their 'national' military service. This was not really a 'feudal' obligation, but a duty to the community pre-dating the feudal structure that had developed in Scotland and England since the eleventh century. The weakness of this system had been demonstrated at several battles during the first War of Independence. Whenever an 'invasion' army encountered a 'defensive' army, for example at Myton or Falkirk, the latter invariably destroyed the former. The greater proportion of experienced and competent soldiers likely to be found in an invasion army compared to a general host called out for the defence of the nation was bound to make the invading force more manageable in every way and more than off-set a disparity in numbers.

The superior articulation, and perhaps motivation, of an invading army may have given commanders a better chance of winning battles, but victories were not necessarily bought at a trivial cost to the victor. After his defeat of Wallace, the payroll strength of Edward I's army fell by some thousands, but the army (and therefore the prestige and credibility) of Wallace effectively ceased to exist.

The field armies of Scotland and England had many similarities. In terms of the kit carried there would generally be no discernible difference between a Scottish knight, man-at-arms, spearman or archer and their English counterparts. The proportions of different types of soldier within the armies might be radically different, but the troops themselves were equipped to much the same standard. For a century before the Wars of Independence there had been a marked and increasing tendency for land grants in Scotland to be more pre–occupied with economic exploitation than with military service, but under Robert I there had been something of a revival of military service stipulations in both royal and baronial charters. Although the practice of giving land for army service continued to be the most important means of acquiring the services of properly armed and armoured men, Robert I and David II both made 'money feifs' which, in theory at least, were temporary expedients. In due course the king, or occasionally a baron would convert the money feif to a conventional land grant when an appropriate property became available.

A great lordship or earldom might be held for the service of several knights, but many small estates were held for fractions of the service of one knight, or for the service of an archer. Fractional service was sometimes shared with a neighbour – particularly when a property was split – or perhaps served on a pro-rata basis; one quarter of a knight's service meaning service for ten days. There are, however examples of land tenure for one eigth or even one twentieth of a knight, which surely indicates a financial burden, fixed in 'real terms' value because the cost of providing a knight was rising, and had been doing so steadily

28. An infantryman, note the particularly heavy mail attached to the helmet to protect the face.

for a long time. By stipulating a price in days rather than a price in money, the grantor was building a hedge against armaments inflation.

Individual soldiers might look the same in either army, but the forces differed in more than just the manner of their recruitment. The example of Dupplin Muir was not lost on Edward III, and archers – particularly mounted archers – became a crucial element in the English approach to battle. The habitual posture of English armies that would be adopted for virtually all their actions in the Hundred Years War was first used on a grand scale at Halidon Hill. There was nothing especially innovative about recruiting archers, they were a vital and integral part of English armies since the Norman Conquest, Edward I's victory at Falkirk had depended on them, but they had not been committed to the battle until the heavy cavalry had been beaten. Before Dupplin, the archers had been an ancillary to the men-at-arms and spearmen. After Dupplin they were an essential element in a combined arms structure where each part of the army depended on the others for survival let alone victory. The traditional perception of English archery needs to be treated with some care. Although there is no doubt that the longbow had a huge influence on English military practice it is easy to become focussed on the archer at the expense of the other constituent parts of English armies. The dominance of the longbow can be seen clearly in the battles of Halidon, Crècy and Poitiers, but without the support of spearmen and men-at-arms the archers were very vulnerable to a fast advance, such as the Scottish cavalry attack at Bannockburn. Because they were isolated from close combat troops who could have protected them from the Scottish cavalry, the archers were scattered by a force undoubtedly very much inferior in numbers.

Furthermore, although the English developed archery to a greater degree than their neighbours, both France and Scotland employed archers in considerable numbers, but neither found that it was necessary to build armies reliant on the longbow in order to win wars against the English. Not one of the actions of English civil wars in this period was a longbow battle. This is not to say that there were not large numbers of archers involved in the actions, but rather that none of those battles was decided by the arrow, they were all decided by a horrendous close-quarters struggle, generally on foot.

A certain amount of 'Robin Hood' inspired mythology has grown up around the longbow. The accuracy and high rate of shooting that could be achieved by a skilled archer made the longbow an awesome weapon, but only a small proportion of men could aspire to that level of skill. When archers were deployed by the thousand, the marksmanship of the individual counted for very little, what mattered was the concentration of arrows landing in a relatively small target area crammed full of the enemy. If the archers of a field army were not sufficiently numerous to make accuracy a secondary consideration compared to concentration, their effect on the battle as a whole would fall a long way short of the arrow storms of Halidon or Poitiers. The defensive army raised in the north of England for the Neville's Cross campaign included at least 1000 archers, and they played an important part in the action, but it is clear that they were not the key feature in the decision of the English commanders to offer battle.

The power of archery to dominate combat was limited by a number of factors. The rate of ammunition consumption could be very high and a man could only carry a very limited supply of arrows and archery is exhausting to perform. Men who made their livings as archers in the service of the crown or great lords practised their art assiduously because both life and livelihood depended their abilities. Those who were called from a civil occupation to serve as archers were unlikely to have anything like the skill or endurance of their more bellicose colleagues. An army recruited across the country for an offensive in Scotland or France could be much more selective in its choice of soldiers than a defensive army enlisted locally. The armies enlisted for these projects were not necessarily much different in numbers, nor in the equipment carried by the men, but an offensive army would have had a far better average level of properly equipped and experienced soldiers.

Even the best of archers was at the mercy of the weather. Even the lightest rain would slow the arrows, compromising both accuracy and penetrative power. A headwind would slow the arrow, though not very badly due to the aerodynamic efficiency of the missile, and a tail wind might help to maintain velocity, but a crosswind would reduce accuracy and velocity. The ratio of surface area to weight in the side elevation of an arrow is enormous compared to the same ratio expressed for 'the business end'. Even a light breeze will push the arrow off target, and make it lose the forward momentum needed to penetrate several layers of protection and still inflict an incapacitating or deadly wound.

Although archers appear regularly in both Scottish and English documentary record, they do not seem to have played a major role in the approach to battle for either side in the small battles that were typical of the war, although both countries were capable of mustering considerable numbers of them. In France the English archers were much more prominent than their counterparts serving in Scotland, which may be a reflection on the higher incidence of wet and windy days in more northerly climes. All the same they were a vital part of the armoury of both armies. The English garrisons invariably included archers on the ration strength. Two men killed at the siege of Perth were described as 'leaders' of the Scottish archers. It is possible that in the day-to-day conduct of the war the most important role of the archer was his contribution in a siege rather than in field operations. The small actions that comprised most of the fighting were not, in any case, the ideal application for archers. Soldiers cannot spend the day on the march with their bows strung and an arrow nocked ready to shoot. Apart from the physical strain on the archer it would ruin the bow. The minute or so that it might take an archer to get ready for action would be of no concern during the manoeuvring of large forces preparing for a general engagement, but it could easily be a minute too long when one was the target of a sudden, unexpected attack.

There is a widely held view that Scottish archers used a shorter bow than their English counterparts but there seems to be no contemporary evidence support this. When a Scottish army was deployed to France in the early fifteenth century it included a very large proportion of archers, but none of the contemporary writers mention short bows. The fact that the Scots won an archery contest against the English in France, during a truce, would surely indicate that even if the Scots *did* use a different bow, it was not a markedly less effective weapon.

Apart from archery, the similarities of Scottish and English armies probably outweigh the differences, at least in operational terms. The largest combatant group

29. Even with relatively short spears, the three ranks of an infantry formation can all participate in combat.

in both armies was usually the spearmen. In a raiding army the spearmen might be mounted, but there was no question of them fighting on horseback. Their animals, like the archers, were intended solely to allow them to keep up with the cavalry. As often as not, the men-at-arms would be fighting dismounted as well, possibly as a separate unit from the spearmen, but probably distributed among them. The drawback to filling the front ranks of the formation with the best-armoured troops would be in keeping the rest of the formation committed to the battle if the first ranks were having a hard time. If the men-at-arms were deployed as a discreet unit they could be used as a subtracted reserve to shore up breaches in line of battle or to exploit any mistakes or misfortunes of the enemy. If the men-at-arms served alongside the spearmen in combat, they could fulfil a 'junior leader' function, encouraging the troops and ensuring they maintain their formation.

English armies had a rank hierarchy in the infantry formations. A *vintenar* was responsible for a group of twenty men and five of these groups were combined into a unit commanded by a *centenar* who in turn came under the command of a *Millenar*, responsible for ten *centenars* in a discrete formation.

More often than not Scottish forces fought either with the entire force on horseback or none at all, and very often as just a single unit. There is no documentary evidence to indicate a formal Scottish command structure, but some structure must have existed for ration parties if nothing else. There certainly was some sort of articulation in Scottish armies, Alan Boyd and John Stirling (not to be confused with the Scottish knight in English service Sir John de Strivelyn or Stirling), killed at Perth were leaders of archers. It would be unreasonable to assume that there was a rank structure for archers alone.

Maintaining formation was vital to battlefield success, but what sort of formation? Wallace arrayed his army at Falkirk in four *schiltroms*, ring formations of spearmen. Likened to a hedgehog, these formations were virtually invulnerable to close attack, and training the men can hardly have been very difficult, but manoeuvring the formation was slow and difficult, and presented a splendid target for archers. The Scots were quite capable of deploying in whatever way they felt was most appropriate to the situation. A schiltrom was not of a particular size or shape, it was merely a column, line or ring formation of close order infantry.

In the heat of hand-to-hand combat that decided almost every action in the medieval period, how did people tell friend from foe? As long as formations remained intact this was probably not too much of a problem. The spearman in the ranks was tightly embedded in among the people he had trained and marched with. If they were on either side of him and he was facing in the same direction as everyone else around him, the spearman was pretty much bound to be facing toward the enemy. Dressing retainers in livery does not seem to have been a common practice, but we should be wary of dismissing it outright. The poet Barbour tells of one of the conspirators against Robert I as having a large number of men in his livery. Barbour was of course writing a poem, and not until after David II's release, but 'livery' was obviously a term and concept perfectly familiar to a Scottish audience of the 1360s or 1370s, so there is no good reason to assume that the Scots of 1340s and 1350s did not provide their retainers with clothing of a given colour. In the small forces employed by both sides throughout most of the

30. Medieval soldiers would have worn similar garments under their armour.

war, correct identification was probably not a great problem because people recognised one another. In a force of fifty or 100 men it would not take long to become familiar with the appearance of everyone in the group. Heraldry might be of value as a means of seeking out some prominent individual, possibly an issue when personal leadership in combat was so important, but was not a great contribution to battlefield identification.

At worst, the spearman might have no physical protection at all; at best he might have a steel cap, armoured gloves and protective coat or shirt. The coat might be of chainmail, but more commonly of leather (preferably boiled in wax, which produces a remarkably tough material) or of cloth stuffed with wool or covered in pitch. Either form of body armour had advantages and disadvantages. Chainmail shirts are, unsurprisingly, rather heavy and the full weight is borne on the shoulders. To make the best of the protective value of the shirt it is necessary to wear a padded garment – a 'gambeson' underneath which obviously adds to the burden and traps heat. Chainmail only really protects the wearer against cuts. The force of the blow from a sword or polearm could break bones through mail without breaking it. The response of archery to the increasingly widespread use of heavy infantry was the 'bodkin' arrowhead, an extremely narrow head that could penetrate chainmail very efficiently. The response to the bodkin was for the infantry to wear yet another layer of protection on top of a mail shirt. This would consist of a jacket, often sleeveless, made from leather or cloth and stuffed with wool padding to reduce the velocity of arrows before they met the chainmail and the protective gambeson beneath it.

The best quality armours no longer relied so heavily on the flexibility and comparative lightness of chainmail. The increasing cost of knight service in the thirteenth century had been on account of the development of plate armour pieces to supplement chainmail. At the beginning of the thirteenth century a man could reasonably be considered properly equipped if he wore a chainmail shirt and hood, a closed helmet and a gambeson in addition to his weapons. At the end of the same century he would also require steel plate arm guards (vambraces), shin guards (greaves), and a breastplate at the very least.

Even a very short period of vigorous exercise in a suit of armour of any description will make the wearer uncomfortably hot even on a cold day. Since the majority of war activity took place in the summer months the wearer could easily succumb to exhaustion in the course of a short fight. On the other hand chainmail affords good protection and is tremendously flexible. Movement is rather easier than might be expected and minor repairs can be made quickly without recourse to a specialist armourer. Leather and cloth armours were considerably lighter and much cheaper, but offered less protection, particularly to arrows, and were not really much less cumbersome than chainmail.

The strain of wearing armour is a thorny issue for historians. The conventional picture as seen in almost any school text book is misleading in the extreme. The idea that an armoured man could not pick himself up if he fell over or mount his horse without the aid of a block and tackle and a set of sheerlegs defies common sense. The men who wore the kit into action were accustomed to the weight, and self evidently no one in their right mind would join battle wearing armour that

31. A jack like this might be worn on top of chainmail as a protection against arrows.

32. Light chainmail hauberk.

would incapacitate them if they happened to lose their footing. None the less, armour of any kind *was* a very real burden and it is unrealistic to assume that anybody could simply slip it on and go into action. If the wearer was going to be an effective combatant he would have to train regularly. This would be especially true for men-at-arms. The addition of steel plates to reinforce vulnerable areas which had become commonplace by the early fourteenth century meant that 'state of the art' battlefield armour was heavier than in any other period, but the weight was not greatly different to the burdens of a modern soldier, and a modern soldier is expected to be able duck, crawl, run, wade through rivers and even climb mountains as well as fight. The consequence of the increasing weight of body armour was the extension of the use of horses, not so much for joining battle – the fourteenth century soldier almost always fought on foot in general engagements – but to carry the troops to the battlefield.

Putting the infantry on horseback reduced the fatigue factor and increased the general mobility of forces by enabling the infantry to travel at the same speed as the cavalry, which meant that small formations could dominate much larger areas than would otherwise be the case. The ease with which even quite large forces could deploy from horseback to dismounted line of battle (like the Scots at Myton) or recover their horses for the pursuit of a broken enemy (as the English did at Neville's Cross) indicates that these manoeuvres were a normal item in the repertoire of both English and Scottish armies.

Our perceptions of the tactical role of heavy cavalry in the medieval period is

33. Closed helmets in the style worn by this man-at-arms were becoming less fashionable in the late thirteenth and early fourteenth centuries.

34. The 'poor bloody infantry' of fourteenth century warfare.

often coloured by a tendency to compare it with the practices of armoured warfare in the twentieth century without having a very clear understanding of either the methodology, practicalities or equipment involved in either. The tank and the knight are both intended to be used in headlong, shock attacks, but only when that is an appropriate response in a particular situation. The men in these formations may not have had the opportunity to train as a unit to any great extent, but they knew what was expected of them – the evolutions of the unit would not have to be particularly intricate. When they did charge, they probably did so at the trot rather than the gallop. In order to make the greatest impression on the enemy it was crucial to have as many men as possible arrive 'on target' at the same moment for obvious reasons, but not at the expense of losing control of the formation. The last thing that the unit could afford would be the high-velocity rugby scrum beloved of romantic Victorian painters. Any collision between ranks would be likely to unhorse at least one rider if not both, and collisions between ranks or files could easily result in horses tripping and forming a veritable pile-up in front of the enemy. The single most important goal for even the most romantic and chivalric inclined man-at-arms in a fight was ensuring his own survival. Not only would he choose not to find himself at the bottom of a heap of his fellows if he could possibly avoid it, but he would not be in a hurry to sacrifice his horse by galloping the creature onto the spearpoints of the enemy infantry. A fully armoured man left behind without his horse as the rest of the formation moved on would be very vulnerable indeed to enemy infantry and no less so to cavalry.

The majority of the time spent in action would not be rapid advances to contact, but in much more sedate roles; reconnaissance, convoy escort, raiding and foraging parties but perhaps most importantly, providing the vanguard when approaching the enemy and protecting the rear when evading him. Since medieval armies were generally formed to carry out one operation in a short period of time – i.e. find the enemy, engage him and destroy his army before the troops indentures are discharged or the money for wages gives out – the task of finding the enemy and keeping him in view while obstructing *his* reconnaissance and foraging was quite a burden, and it fell most heavily on men-at-arms.

For some, those demands were what brought them to Scotland in the first place. Nothing was more fashionable among the upper classes as soldiering. To fight manfully in a foreign war was the mark of a man of the world, and the war in Scotland could certainly offer plenty of opportunities to fight, though not in great battles of manoeuvre. Indeed, since the actions were so small, it would be easier for chivalrous behaviour to be observed and noted than in a large action There was little point in risking life and limb for glory and honour if no-one was going to notice.

The tactical practices adopted in large battles are reasonably well understood, but those of small battles are not so clearly documented. It would be misleading to assume that the same considerations hold true for both sorts of engagements.

35. Infantry combat.

Throughout the period between Halidon Hill and Neville's Cross – fourteen years of war interspersed with truces of short duration – there were no major battles, and most of the actions that did occur were encounter battles, where mounted infantry and the men-at-arms probably ruled the day. The amount of time needed for the mounted archers that were such an important constituent of English forces in particular to deploy usefully would be an obstacle to their effective use against an enemy making an unexpected appearance. This was not universally the case. The battle of Culblean in November 1335 would seem to be very much in the convention of Scottish military practice in major engagements– a large battle writ small – but mostly such combat as took place between Halidon in 1333 and Neville's Cross in 1346 consisted of running fights and ambushes.

Even the very best of armours did not render the wearer entirely safe in combat. The purpose of armour was to protect the body if an assailant could get past one's 'guard' – one's sword and shield – and to reduce the risk of arrow wounds; it did not turn the wearer into a sort of medieval tank, it just gave him great advantage over an unarmoured opponent. There is no reason to assume that any of these armours could not be produced locally, but the large-scale import of weapons and armour both in England and Scotland suggests that the demand for equipment was greater than could be satisfied by local craftsmen. Despite the repeated instructions of English kings from Edward I onwards arms were exported from England to Scotland, sometimes as re-exports through Irish ports. The risks to merchants involved in this trade were high, so the potential for profit must have been very good to make it worthwhile.

6
TURNING THE TIDE

When Edward III disbanded his army at Perth at the close of his summer offensive of 1335 he had some cause to believe that his Scottish war was at last beginning to bear fruit. He had been able to move his troops beyond the Forth with little opposition and had captured the Scottish guardian, the Earl of Moray. He had offered amnesty to Bruce supporters that had been reasonably well received and had felt sufficiently confident about the military situation to leave his lieutenants and Edward Balliol to complete the process of making peace with the Scots while he returned to England. Balliol had moved north to confront the Bruce party in their northern heartland with a modest but powerful and highly mobile column of troops that would be the foundation of an army to be raised from Balliol sympathisers in Badenoch, Atholl and Buchan which he could reasonably expect to mop up any continuing resistance through the capture of such castles as remained in Bruce hands.

By the middle of October he had appointed two Scottish Balliol supporters – the priest William Bullock and Sir Alexander Mowbray, the latter just recently returned to the Balliol party – to conduct negotiations with the rump of the Bruce party, now led by Sir Andrew Moray, the former guardian, who had been ransomed from the English in 1334 to the dismay of Edward Balliol.

A truce had been granted to the Scots for three weeks from 22 October 1335 to allow the talks to continue. The precise conditions of the truce are unknown, but it seems to have been restricted to certain areas of Scotland; Edward Balliol was still conducting offensive operations in the north against the Bruce party until October, when he returned to Perth, leaving David de Strathbogie to continue the campaign. Strathbogie was determined to break the back of the opposition once and for all by forcing free tenants off the land and replacing them with Balliol sympathisers, a further indication that the truce did not extend to the whole of the country.

36. Personal possesions - a dagger, rosary, flint and steel and a pair of dice.

The truce was renewed several times and was eventually prolonged to Christmas 1335 with the provision that Scots who had not yet made their peace with the Balliol/Plantagenet administration would have to do so on or before 26 November if they were to be automatically guaranteed continuity of tenure and safety of life and limb. Those who failed to do so might be provided for in the outcome of the current negotiations but there was no absolute guarantee that the discussions would come to anything, but there must have been some confidence that agreement would be reached. One of the issues discussed was the provision of estates for the exiled king David, and a commission was set up to measure out the lands that would in the future provide a suitable income for himself and his wife, who, as the sister of Edward III could not be left penniless.

Possibly Edward III was confident that the issues of Scottish and his possession of the southern counties could be resolved politically without his presence, because he had retired to Northumberland, but the fact that he was prepared to negotiate at all perhaps suggests that he felt that continuing his military efforts might be politically counter-productive as well as financially difficult. The recent campaign had restored his fortunes and those of the Disinherited, but the Bruce party had recovered from several thorough defeats in the past. If he could not bring about a political settlement that would have the support of the vast majority of Scots of all persuasions there was every danger that the pattern of successful English invasions followed by equally successful Scottish recoveries could go on indefinitely. Sooner or later it would become impossible to recruit men or to find

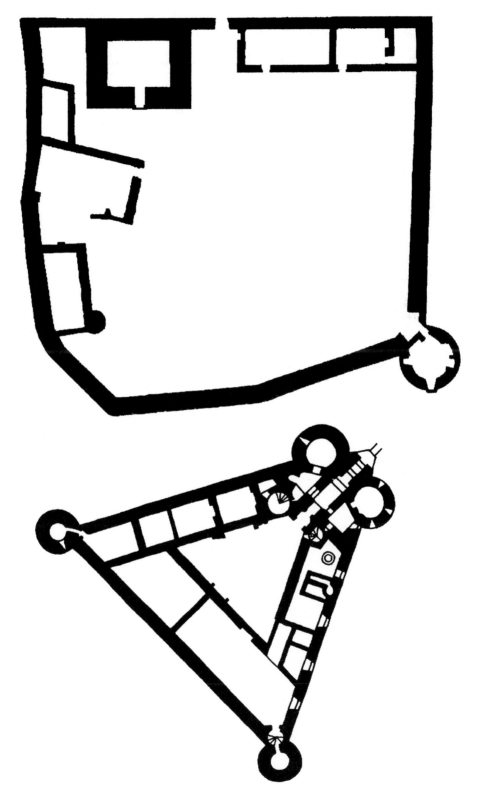

37. Outline maps of the walls of (*top*) Lochleven Castle and (*bottom*) Caerlaverock Castle.

the money to continue a war which was already proving to be an obstruction to his intentions in France.

Edward III had moved his household to Alnwick by the beginning of November and any doubts he may have had about the value of the discussions with the Scots which were taking place at Bathgate, just south of the Forth were justified by reports from David de Strathbogie that the Balliol position in the north was deteriorating rapidly. Before the end of the month Edward had decided that the situation warranted instructions for a levy of troops from the north-east of England, presumably with a view to armed intervention in support of Balliol and Strathbogie's forces.

Bruce power in the north of Scotland centred on Kildrummy castle, commanded by Lady Christian Bruce, the sister of King Robert and wife of Sir Andrew Moray. Realising that he could not hope to dominate the region so long as the castle was held against him, Strathbogie laid siege to it.

Andrew Moray was in the midst of negotiations with Sir William Montagu, who had been closely involved in English operations in Scotland since the Halidon Hill campaign. Despite the current truce, which may not, after all, have applied in the north of Scotland, Strathbogie was obviously carrying on with the fight, so Moray would not have been contravening it by moving north to defend his wife and their property. It would seem that he asked Montagu for a temporary adjournment of the peace negotiations and for permission to seek out Strathbogie.

38. Boots and shoes were quite flimsy – armies on the march must have become extremely footsore.

39. Man-at-arms and an infantryman.

Montagu was prepared to accede to Moray's request, possibly for no better reason than because it would be the knightly, and therefore 'proper', thing to do. This unlikely-sounding arrangement should not be discounted out of hand. Men (and women) of rank could be quite serious about behaving in an honourable and chivalrous fashion to their enemies, especially if they felt that their own reputations as 'flowers of chivalry' could be damaged if they behaved otherwise. Montagu may, however, have given his permission for more practical reasons. The Scots had not been eager to meet the English in battle for some time. Their unwillingness to fight had been a factor in the failure of the two Edwards to end the war. If Moray went north to meet Strathbogie, he would have to take a considerable proportion of the remaining military strength of the Scots with him.

Patrick Dunbar, Earl of March and lord William Douglas brought their 'ledings' or retinues to the expedition. The numbers were small, but these would have been the 'the floure of that half the Scottish se'(the best troops in Scotland south of the Firth of Forth) as the Scottish chronicler Wyntoun describes them. If Sir Andrew was beaten by Strathbogie he and his adherents might well be killed or taken prisoner, and even if they were not, one more defeat for the Bruce party could very probably result in the final disintegration of their support in the community.

At the very least any force that accompanied Moray on his expedition would effectively denude the Bruce party south of the Forth of armed men for at least as long as it took to find Strathbogie, fight him and then return to the south, during which time the English and Balliol troops should have been able to improve their position. If Moray could be comprehensively beaten, the end of the war would be in sight.

Montagu, then, had some reason to be optimistic about this turn of events. Sufficiently so that he does not seem to have felt it was desirable to dispatch any reinforcements to Strathbogie, but that assumes that he had troops to spare. Although Moray took a force of 800 men with him (according to the chronicler John of Fordoun) this may not have represented the full strength of the Bruce party in the lowlands. If so, Montagu may have feared a new outbreak of fighting in the south that could swamp the garrisons if he stripped them of men in support of an operation in the north which might after all come to nothing. He may also have believed that there were political considerations. If Moray was beaten by a force under Strathbogie that could be described as 'Scottish', there could be positive dividends in diplomatic terms. The diplomatic campaign of Edward III at the *curia* depended largely on describing the war in Scotland as a domestic problem in the kingdom of Edward III's vassal. As long as all the fighting was essentially between English and Scottish forces it was impossible for English diplomats to maintain that position with any credibility. Even if a sizeable portion of Strathbogie's army had been drawn from the retinues of English magnates or were English soldiers in the

40. Plate armour became increasingly popular throughout the fourteenth century.

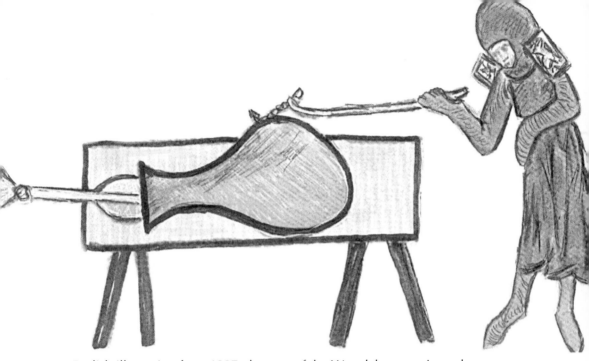

1. English illustration from 1327, the year of the Weardale campaign, when, according to the poet Barbour, 'crakkes of were' (cracks of war) were used for the first time.

2. Fourteenth-century cavalrymen would carry a much heavier lance.

Opposite   3. A liveried archer. Livery was becoming increasingly common by the mid-fourteenth century.

4. Monument at Culblean battlefield. Photo: Jim Anderson

Opposite   5. A fully armoured soldier.
6. & 7. A helmet with chainmail guards in detail and (*below*) in battle.

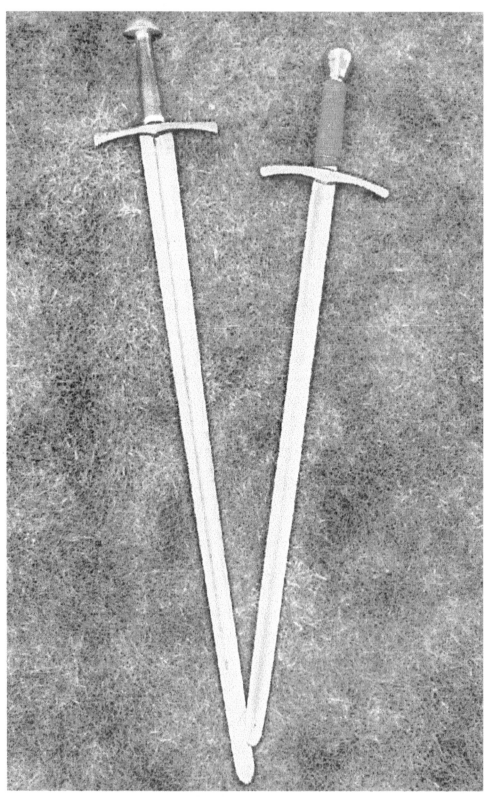

8. Swords, always a secondary weapon after the lance or polearm but still a crucial part of a soldiers equipment.

9. An 'irn hat' or *chapel de fer*.

10. Infantry, in this case Scots, but English or French troops would look very similar.

Opposite   11. Arming for battle, possible on your own but easier with assistance.
Note the thickness of the padded jacket.

12. Caerlaverock castle.

13. Machicolation.

14. A jack might be worn over chainmail or underneath it.

15. The links of this chainmail shirt are much the same diameter as those in the illustration above, but the gauge of metal is heavier.

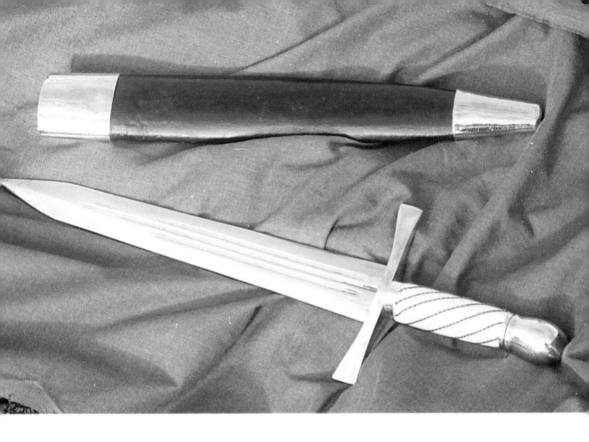

16. A dagger, an essential part of the soldiers equipment.

17. A reconstruction of a trebuchet, a permanent exhibit at Caerlaverock Castle.

Opposite   18. Note the padded trousers of this infantryman.

19. A bow and arrows, a crucial aspect of fourteenth-century wafare.

20. Light archers.

21. Stringing a bow.

22. Few soldiers aspired to such a grand tent – most would sleep in the open air or in billets.

Overleaf   23. The view north from Stirling Castle

41. An example of an early barbute or bascinet helmet. Note also the leather bracer to protect the wrist while shooting a bow.

42. Even in lowland areas terrain could prove difficult, river gorges aford dead ground
routes even in the good agricultural areas of eastern Scotland.

service of a Scottish magnate the propaganda value of the victory would be a boon
for the diplomatic struggle for foreign recognition of Edward Balliol as King of
Scots. Edward III's diplomats would be better able to present the war as an internal
Scottish conflict in which Edward was acting in defence of his vassal, rather than
conducting a war of conquest in support of a pretender.

The men that marched northward with Moray were chiefly the retinues of earls
and barons from the southern counties. A policy of pushing free tenants off the land
that had been adopted by Strathbogie in the north had also been employed in the
ceded counties of the south. Men who were threatened with the loss of their estates
as a result of Balliol/Plantagenet victory had little to lose by following their lords –
equally threatened – in an attempt to frustrate the advance of the Balliol cause in the
north-east. Their best hope of future prosperity lay with the Bruce party and If there
was to be any chance of reversing the fortunes of that party generally, the reservoir
of manpower and wealth in the north that the Bruce party had depended on since
the first Balliol invasion would have to be preserved. Without it there was very little
likelihood that the Bruce party would be able to recover anywhere else.

Moray was pursuing the Bruce interest, but he was also protecting his own lordship
and his authority as guardian. If he was unable to provide 'good lordship' for his own
tenants and neighbours, if he was unable to offer them stability and security, his
credibility as guardian would be compromised. If Moray lost the guardianship, his
replacement might be more inclined to come to terms with the English and Edward
Balliol, and those terms might not be too careful of the rights of Moray himself.

While Moray led his column north, Strathbogie decided to move on his enemy rather than await his appearance at Kildrummy. He made his way south through the Boultenstone pass and camped his force somewhere to the north and east of Loch Davan intending to force an engagement as quickly as possible before Moray had the opportunity to gather any more troops. He was too late. A detachment of men from the Kildrummy garrison, which must have set out in search of the relief force almost as soon as Strathbogie had lifted the siege, was already marching toward Moray, whose troops had reached the hall of Logie Ruthven. Strathbogie had gained the tactical advantage of being able to deploy on higher ground than his enemy while still dominating the path to Kildrummy. Moray could not proceed further without either attacking uphill – an unattractive proposition given the experiences of Dupplin and Halidon – or exposing his flank or rear if he tried to by-pass his enemy and make straight for Kildrummy.

While they were camped at the hall of Logie Ruthven, Moray, March and Douglas, possibly already joined by the Earl of Ross, were reinforced by a detachment from the garrison of Kildrummy castle under John Craig of Auchindoir. Craig was able to show Moray a path along which his forces could approach Strathbogie unseen. Passing some distance from Strathbogie's pickets they were able to take up a position uphill and to the west of his army. Although this march was made in the dark preparatory to a dawn attack, the distance involved was only about three miles and the majority of the troops would have been mounted, so it need not have taken very long to perform. The Scots dismounted, secured their horses and divided into two units, one under Douglas and the other under Moray, and advanced. It was not, however done quickly enough to compromise Strathbogie's sentries and he had enough warning to be able to form his troops to face the Scottish formation under the command of Douglas that was approaching him. Seeing that the advantage of surprise had been lost Douglas halted his force on the south-facing slope above a ford in the burn o'vat, a small stream that runs west down Culblean Hill into Loch Kinnord. Strathbogie seized the moment and ordered his men forward, thinking that the enemy had had a crisis of morale. As his men charged they lost their formation and Douglas counter-charged just as the remainder of the Scots under Moray appeared on his flank. The result was a crushing defeat for Balliol interests in the north. Strathbogie had been killed in the battle and he had no heir old enough to pursue his claim to the earldom of Atholl. Edward Balliol had lost an effective lieutenant and could not replace him. He could of course invest someone else with the *title* of Earl of Atholl, but if it had been difficult for David de Strathbogie, who could make a coherent claim to the earldom by reasons of legitimate descent and enjoyed some local sympathy, to enforce his lordship, it would be virtually impossible for anyone else to do so.

With no magnate support in the north of the country, and unable to defend his gains in the south without the continual military interventions of Edward III over and above the garrisons of the ceded counties Balliol could not help but look more and more a client of the English and less and less like a king – even a vassal king.

In the spring of 1336, the Scots were able to hold a council at Dunfermline, which re-appointed Sir Andrew Moray as guardian. The fact that they could arrange this meeting so far south and so close to the Balliol garrisons at Perth and

43. Looking north on the battlefield at Culblean where David de Strathbogie was killed.

44. Looking towards Culblean Hill (*left*) across the burn o'vat.

Cupar speaks volumes for their confidence about the military situation. They did not have things all their own way however. Early in 1336 the siege of Cupar was broken by a force from the garrison of Edinburgh castle. The commander of Cupar, the Scottish priest and Edward Balliol's chamberlain, Sir William Bullock, was hard pressed. Edward had appointed John de Stirling, described in Lanercost as a Scottish knight, as governor of Edinburgh castle, and he led a force of forty men-at-arms and eighty archers 'and other men' on a sortie to relieve the garrison of Cupar. The truce, interrupted rather than broken by the battle of Culblean, had been extended to May 1336, and was in theory between Edward III and the Bruce party. It did not apply to the conflict between the Bruce and Balliol parties. Since Edward III was footing the bill for Edward Balliol's army and an enormous programme of castle improvement this might seem like a distinction without a difference, but it presumably it was effected to keep the war out of the north of England, and so was useful to Edward III, and it allowed the Scots to concentrate their efforts on the Garrisons and supporters of Edward Balliol. Truces were generally quite well observed, but there was always the risk that the enemy might break a truce in the hope of destroying the enemy in one sharp fight.

Edward Balliol's position was becoming untenable once again. If Edward III wanted to make good the promises of Edward Balliol to cede him the Sherrifdoms and Constabularies of the southern counties he was going to have to mount another campaign in Scotland if only to demonstrate his confidence in the eventual success of his vassal. This time Edward mustered his army at Perth and set out on what was essentially a punitive operation throughout north-east Scotland as far as Elgin, where he spared the cathedral and then retiring to Aberdeen. Aberdeen was the commercial mainstay of the Bruce party, the only important town and harbour in their hands. Not surprisingly, Edward burnt it to the ground before moving south again to Perth.

He had evidently decided that his Scottish hopes depended on the security of the towns and castles in his or Edward Balliol's possession. The defences of Perth were upgraded, including the erection of stone walls on three sides and three towers, the cost being imposed on six monasteries in the region. The castles of Leuchars and St Andrews in fife were rebuilt by Henry Ferrers and Henry Beaumont. Edward gave instructions for the refortification of Dunottar, Kyneff and Lauriston castles and for improvements to Stirling and Edinburgh. The financial stress of this campaign must have been immense. According to the Lanercost Chronicle, Edward was carrying the full burden of wages and supplies for Edward Balliol's army. He was able to grace his 1336 campaign with an act of chivalry. Katherine Beaumont, the widow of David de Strathbogie, was under siege in Lochindorb castle. Edward mounted a successful operation to lift the siege, but had great difficulty keeping his men and horses fed due to the scorched earth tactics employed by Moray. Leaving a strong force in Perth with Edward Balliol, Edward made his way to Bothwell, where he enlarged the garrison and ordered refortification to be completed through the winter.

45. Even very poor men were expected to have a spear or a bow.

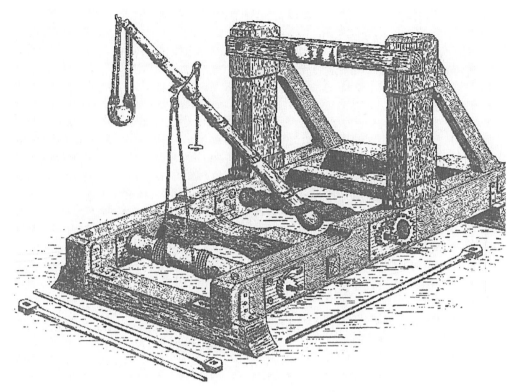

46. A catapult. After Payne-Gallway.

These activities did him little good. Sir Andrew Moray carried the war to the enemy relentlessly from the autumn of 1336 through to the spring of 1337. The castles of Dunottar, Kinneff and Lauriston seem to have fallen to the Scots quite quickly, suggesting that the various refurbishments ordered by Edward III had not been completed before the Scots were able to seize these strongholds. Edward Balliol did not sit idly behind the new fortifications at Perth. He committed the force that he had been entrusted with by Edward III to a series of operations in the Mearns, Angus and the Carse of Gowrie against the forces of Moray. He does not seem to have been able to secure the region from the enemy, but the whole area was ruined by the continual fighting. This may have denied the territory to the Scots, but it can hardly have made it an asset for the Balliol government since little or no revenue can have been raised to support his administration.

Early in 1337 Moray had moved the focus of the war into Fife, capturing and destroying minor castles and threatening the viability of the Balliol cause north of the Forth other than in the immediate environs of strongholds such as Perth, Cupar and St Andrews. Even these were not safe. The Scots had mastered the technology of effective siege artillery and no longer had to conduct a long, close siege to starve out a garrison. Even the first-class castle at St Andrews capitulated after an investment of only three weeks. Since St Andrews could be supplied by sea, it is reasonable to conclude that the surrender was prompted by the destruction of the walls and towers inflicted by a weapon called 'boustour' which figures in Scottish accounts.

Edward Balliol in Perth and Edward III in Bothwell were unable to prevent the Scots from continuing their offensive. Moray could take the field securely, aware that his enemy had no army with which to confront him. This probably says more about the weakness of the two Edwards than it does about the strength of Moray. Even if the Scottish army amounted to no more than 1000 men, the combined households and garrisons of the two Edwards were evidently not sufficient to warrant offering battle or even an active resistance. Of course, if their cause did not enjoy the sympathy of the community, it would be both difficult and futile to risk troops in delaying or spoiling actions. If local sympathies lay with the Bruce party, or were even just against the Balliol party, the benefit of local knowledge and intelligence to conduct such actions successfully would be hard to come by.

St Andrews' castle fell to Moray's army at the end of February. He was engaged in besieging Bothwell before the end of March, and it had fallen before the end of lent. Edward had scoured Scotland in search of an enemy to fight. Now the enemy was in the field, but he did not have enough of an army for the task. Abandoning Bothwell castle, he returned to England, determined that his Parliament would provide money for a new campaign, but not in Scotland.

Making war in Scotland was a hard and dangerous business in uncomfortable surroundings, and it was beginning to look like it would never yield a profit. The scorched earth policies of Scottish tradition may have been applied with unusual severity in 1336/37. Chronicle records stress the extent of the destruction of Angus and the Mearns, and then Fife and Lanarkshire as the Scottish army made its way from one castle to the next. Even if the English won another crushing victory over the Scots, would it bring peace any closer? In 1333 Edward had hoped to acquire a great deal of territory through a short war that would place his candidate on the throne of a smaller Scotland. Instead he had spent vast sums on endless money-pit campaigns to protect a clutch of counties in the south of Scotland that would produce little or no revenue for years – certainly not enough to warrant such continuous expenditure and service in Scotland was losing its allure for the men who led Edward's troops. Men who had claims on estates in Scotland could be relied on to bear arms against the Scots as long as Edward could find their wages; for those without Scottish prospects, the wages were not enough of an inducement of themselves for people who might have to find heavy sum for their ransom if they were captured. The king would very possibly promise a contribution toward release, but it might be a long time coming.

If Edward wanted to continue his military career without making himself bankrupt he would have to fight in a more profitable environment. He spent spring and summer of 1337 preparing for an invasion of France.

An English army of sorts was maintained in Scotland under the Earl of Warwick, Thomas Beauchamp, but the army for the French expedition was bound to have priority. Despite the many English garrisons scattered throughout Scotland and a field army which at its peak was over 3000 strong Beauchamp could not prevent the Scots under Sir Andrew Moray from raiding beyond the ceded counties of southern Scotland and into the north of England. His field force reduced to just 300 he had to shelter in Carlisle from the Scots in October.

Moray made no attempt on Carlisle. Instead he took his army to Edinburgh and joined or commenced a siege on the castle, recently re-built by Edward III and a vital part of his administrative and military structure for the English pale that he was striving for. The loss of Edinburgh would be a severe blow, so a force was raised from English marches and sent north to relieve the garrison and drive off the Scots. The castle did not fall at this time, the Scots moved south to meet their enemy.

The Scots raised the siege and came to meet them at Clerkington, the English being at Crichton, where at Crichtondene there was a fierce encounter between them, many being slain on both sides, but the English lost the most

Thomas Grey, Scalacronica

Crichtondene was not a conclusive victory for the Scots, but they would seem to have had the better of it. The Scottish army moved south to Galashiels, threatening the north of England, but the English army managed to confront them somewhere on the north bank of the Tweed and thus prevent their advance. The two armies faced one another for two days, unwilling or unable to offer battle before dispersing.

Although Edward was obviously preoccupied with the impending attack on France, he did not abandon the Scottish front. Apart from the all too obvious military necessity of conducting an offensive in Scotland, Edward had to be seen doing something about his Scottish problems if his parliament was going to be prepared to foot the bill for his new war in France. The earls of Salisbury and Arundel had replaced the Earl of Warwick around the end of 1337. By the 13 January they had started to lay siege to Dunbar castle. The castle's owner was Patrick, Earl of March. He had been a supporter of Edward Balliol and a paid retainer of Edward III in 1332/33, but had defected to the Bruce party in 1335. The castle had been rebuilt at least partly at the expense of Edward III during the period when the Earl had been in his fealty. In the intervening period the Earl had been actively involved in the Scottish campaigns, but his Castle does not seem to have been threatened until 1338. The defence of the castle was left to the countess of March, Agnes Randolph. Her response to the missiles that struck the castle wall was to have a young woman dressed as a bride go to the point of impact and lightly 'dust away' the damage – an inspired application of psychological warfare. The siege continued for five months before the English army abandoned it. The Scots had been able to deliver provisions and a reinforcement of forty men-at-arms into the castle from the sea and the English artillery had not battered the garrison into submission or created a breach in the defences so there was little point in keeping men at Dunbar who could be more useful elsewhere. Failing to capture Dunbar castle was a blow to the credibility of English arms in Scotland. It was followed by another, the defeat of a force of troops from the English marches at Presfen, near Wark-on-Tweed. The Scots were not having it all their own way. The Earl of March led men across the border and was 'discomfited' by a force that included, and was possibly commanded by, Sir Thomas Grey, the English chronicler.

The government of the Bruce party was beset by problems of authority. At the audit of 1337, the chancellor, Sir Adam Buttergask, was accused of withholding

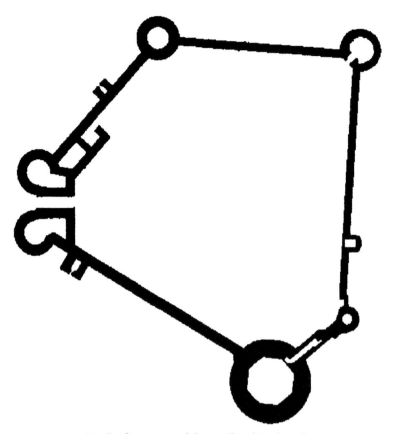

47. Outline map of the walls of Bothwell Castle.

crown revenues. His successful defence was that two magnates, the Steward and Earl of Moray, had lifted the money in question, claiming the authority of the crown. The competition for power that caused this episode is usually perceived as evidence of a state of anarchy, but the king's revenues were obviously being collected and accounted for, it was only the right of a particular person to lift and spend the money that was in dispute. The fact that an audit was held to account for crown revenues at all is a fairly positive indication that the government was surviving the war. If the Balliol administration had ever had a viable existence independent of English support, it had long ceased by the time Perth surrendered to the Scots on 17 August 1339. Although Perth was Balliol's capital when he could maintain a presence there, a great deal of the seven years that had passed since his coronation had been spent in England raising troops to make new attempts on the Scottish crown or else moving around the country trying to establish himself as the rightful wearer of that crown. He had had little chance of building an administration with any depth of acceptance in the community.

The siege of Perth lasted for ten weeks and was a sophisticated business, involving the construction of ditches or tunnels to drain the moat and waterborne attacks by French mercenaries under Hugh Haudpile, whom even a patriotic Scottish writer calls 'a dangerous pirate'. Haudpile would appear to have been trying to cut off the garrison from supply by sea, or possibly storm the town in a surprise attack, but in either case he lost his best ship in the fighting and seems to have had to mount another operation to recover it. The eventual surrender of the garrison was prompted by the fall of Cupar castle to the Scots. William Bullock had been persuaded by Douglas to surrender Cupar and defect to the Scots in exchange for security of life, limb and property. Bullock and Douglas then joined the Steward's siege at Perth and the town surrendered thereafter. Although a priest, Bullock seems to have had an armed following of his own, because he is described as joining the Scots 'with all his men'. Aside from his military and clerical activities, Bullock managed to conduct a remarkable political career. Having served Edward Balliol as chamberlain he later served David Bruce most effectively in the same office. The fall of Cupar and Perth meant there were no English garrisons north of the Forth. The next siege on the agenda was the 'pele' at Stirling – a fortified camp rather than a castle – that Edward III had had constructed as part of his campaign in summer 1336. This proved to be a hard nut to crack, and did not fall to the Scots for a long time. Like Perth, Stirling could be replenished by sea and was not therefore dependent on control of the roads in the way that Cupar or Bothwell were. The war slowed, but did not stop. William Douglas and William Bullock captured Edinburgh castle by a *ruse de guerre*. Disguised as merchants, a party of men-at-arms placed a short tree trunk under the portcullis so that it could not be dropped into place when the alarm was raised.

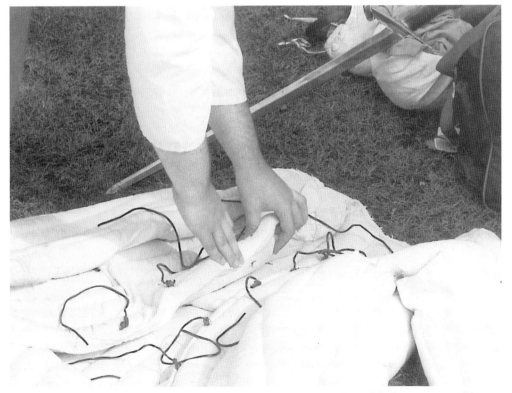

48. Tightly packed with wool, the jack could become unbearably hot very quickly.

49. A bow was effective to a range of around 200 yards.

Once they had secured the gate a party of townspeople came to their support and seized the castle. The initiative lay with the Scots, and Douglas was strong enough to carry his campaign into Teviotdale where he 'expelled from the realm' the remaining English forces.

New leaders were coming to the fore in Scotland. Men like Sir Alexander Ramsay and Sir William Douglas, men who had grown up in the thick of war with the English, established dashing reputations as 'flowers of chivalry'. There were still important English garrisons to be ousted, but the Scots were certainly winning their war. The death through illness of the guardian, Sir Andrew Moray was to some extent offset by the return from English captivity of Sir John Randolph. The time had come to force the pace of the war a little, and Moray, Douglas and Ramsay embarked on increasingly aggressive operations that drove the English off the land or behind castle walls. Even the arrival of Edward III at Melrose in the winter of 1341 failed to make any impression on a war that had slowed to a stalemate between the Scots, masters of everywhere north of the Forth and the English/Balliol forces; struggling to retain authority in some areas of the south.

What Edward could have actually done to change the situation in Scotland is hard to say. He had stopped recruiting large armies for Scottish campaigns partly because of his commitments in France, partly because he just could not afford them, but also because there was little to be achieved with such an army if the Scots would not accept battle. Once such an army had been dismissed, even quite small Scottish forces could quickly regain control of most areas. As long as the Scots maintained their practice of waging a war of small mobile formations

50. A staff sling could shoot a stone around 200 yards. The black blur above the slinger's head is the stone in flight.

there was not really very much for a slow moving invasion force to do. Raiding villages and burning crops could be done just as effectively by much smaller forces, and was counter-productive because it drove Scots who might otherwise have been disinterested or even sympathetic to the Balliol government toward the Bruce party.

The recovery of the Bruce party from the defeat of Halidon and the massive loss of territory and castles thereafter was a slow, but steady, even relentless process. The ascendancy in battle that the Scots attained in the mid 1330s was derived from actions that seem almost trivial in size. Even a significant engagement like Culblean probably involved no more than 3000 people in total, and very probably rather less. Both sides relied increasingly on professionalism rather than numbers to achieve military objectives. The primary objective was the domination of the land – the power to exert lordship. This was best achieved by small units of men well enough armed and mounted to intimidate villagers and small parties of the enemy, but mobile enough to outrun any serious opposition. These formations were very small, most of the time the ledings of even great magnates would be a matter of dozens rather than hundreds. The force that fought against David de Strathbogie at Culblean included the followings of three great lords, Sir Andrew Moray, Douglas and the Earl of March, but it was still a force of only a few hundreds. Far from being a minor scrap, Culblean was an important and tactically decisive battle. Obviously it would have been difficult to forage adequately for a large force in winter, but the speed required if the Scots were going to interrupt

51. A good quality jack gave good protection against blows but comparatively little against cuts.

Strathbogie's siege of Kildrummy called for a mounted force anyway. The scale of forces the Scots took into the field was almost invariably small, so men responsible for choosing who would serve would be as choosy as they could be to ensure that the force that they raised was as competent and as well-equipped as possible. If we are to have a picture of these forces we should perhaps expect to see a body of men, quite heavily armoured, who in general would be more inclined to fight on foot, but on horse if necessary.

The running fight at Burghmuir and Edinburgh that resulted in the capture of the count of Namur, and the encounters at Crichtondene and Presfen show that the Scots were prepared to seek battle on horseback when appropriate and could hold their own. This rather undermines the dearly held tradition that the Scots could to afford to buy or feed the expensive warhorses that were a *sine qua non* of knightly combat. Despite the evolution of heavy infantry and archery, the mounted man-at-arms was still a vital facet of military life. His mobility, his personal skill at arms and the *élan* of the charge was by far the most effective vehicle for projecting power over considerable distances relatively quickly and with few mouths to feed during the operation.

For the wealthy, the best of armour and the best of horses were absolutely vital possessions because the war had become a competitive arena for chivalry-orientated men. Quite apart from the fighting there were spectacular tournaments in which the ambitious could distinguish themselves. If Scots were going to be able to compete they would need to have the right kit. To fight effectively on horseback demands a high level of skill on the part of the rider, but also that man and horse are well accustomed to one another so that they act as a team. Borrowing another man's horse to take part in a tournament was unlikely to be a very rewarding experience.

The Scottish war provided an arena for chivalrous exchanges of pleasantries under safe conducts, but it was also the proving-ground conflict for Edward III's more famous exploits in France. The contract army system that recruited the armies that fought at Crécy and Poitiers was developed for the conquest of Scotland, the combined arms tactical relationship between men-at-arms and archers was refined in the two dramatic victories of Dupplin Muir and Halidon Hill. Most importantly, Scotland was where Edward's commanders learned their trade. Although the Hundred Years War would be dominated by the great longbow victories like Crécy and Poitiers, most of the conflict was conducted by relatively small parties of men; by professionals or at least men for whom military service was a major part of life as opposed to an occasional burden in times of national or regional emergency.

In the close knit local warfare that comprised most military activity, it was relatively easy for an active and able soldier to become a well-known figure in society. Regular victories, however minor, kept the English on the defensive, or at least let the Scots hold the initiative, but fighting well, regardless of whether the engagement was won or lost, could make a man famous. The lucky and skilful few acquired reputations and fortunes. 'Flowers of chivalry' like Ramsay and Douglas could take pride in their achievements in what was perceived at the time to be almost the only really noble and honourable pursuit for a gentleman – fighting.

Their success drew like-minded Scots to their 'schools of chivalry', which sounds very grand, but Ramsay had been making war from his camp in the caves at Hawthornden. The war may have become an arena for the chivalrous classes of both countries, but it was not a frivolous business. A few served out of a sense of adventure or for the honour and prestige of having performed chivalrous exploits, but the majority of men served because of their obligations to the crown and to their landlord. Forty days of each in the course of a year, and possibly extra duty in times of local emergency would constitute a huge demand on the willingness of men to discharge that duty.

7
THE PEOPLE AND THE LAND

When men serve in a war it is largely because some other man tells them to. Men seldom have much influence over when or where they will fight let alone whether or why they should fight at all. This was no less true of medieval society than of our own. Men fought at the instigation and under the direction of the aristocracy that owned the country. For most of them it was probably an imposition that they could easily have lived without. All the same, they did fight, and sometimes they did so despite the orders of their lord rather than because of it. The full range of factors that drew people to fight is too wide a topic for this work, but some of them should at least be mentioned.

In the earlier war of independence the participation of all ranks of society characterises the nature of the struggle. Most people would certainly have preferred a quiet life, so there was obviously something about the English occupation that was deeply and widely enough resented in the community as a whole to encourage people of all ranks to assist the Balliol cause and then the Bruce cause as the most effective force against the rule of Edward I, and then later, Edward II. At the end of the day, men fought out of fear; fear that they would have to pay higher taxes; that they would be forced to perform military service for the English in France, that the decay of servile status in Scotland over the previous 100 years would be reversed, but more than any thing else, the fear that they would lose the land they lived on.

What sort of land was the Second Scottish War of Independence fought over and fought for? A good deal of northern and western Scotland, the mountainous parts, is little changed in appearance since the fourteenth century. Some terms used in medieval documents have changed their popular meaning. Today a forest is an area of woodland, but 700 years ago the connotation was 'wilderness'. The armies that fought the war passed over mountains and through forest when they

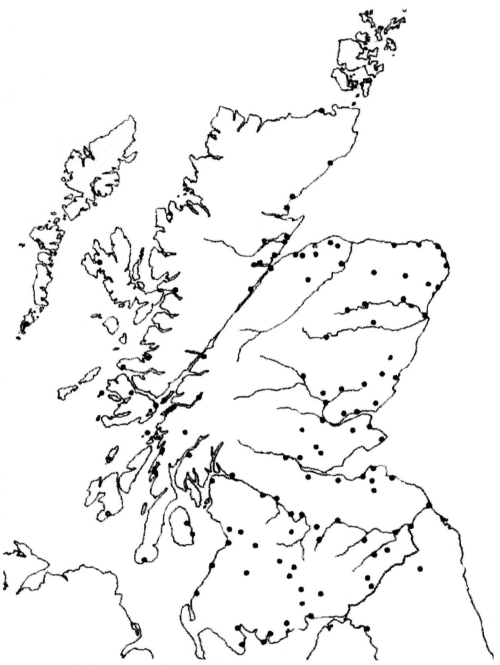

52. Distribution map of castles and military camps in the fourteenth century.

had to, but most campaigning took place in the most densely populated and agriculturally productive parts of the country. The prosperity of the whole community rested on farming, so it is worth examining Scottish society if only to see what the Scots were fighting *for* in their wars with the English. The wars may have been fomented by powerful landowners, but they could not conduct those wars without the support of the community as a whole.

Popular histories of Scotland (and some scholarly ones as well) offer a grim picture of universally impoverished peasant farmers living in the thrall of (probably rapacious) lordly nobles and gentry in a primitive agricultural – largely pastoral – economy; of an instability in medieval Scotland – wars with England, domestic wars, plagues among the people, epidemics among sheep, cattle and even chickens conspiring with poor climate and soil conditions to prevent any real improvement in the wealth of the society. This is not a view supported to any great degree by the archaeological evidence, nor really by the documentary record of the period. Much of our picture of agricultural Scotland is coloured by the fact that so much of the pre-improvement landscape is only described to us by the improvers in their estate plans and in their diaries, letters and most importantly their publications. Improving landlords had an agenda to pursue. Part of the justification for improvement inevitably lay in criticising the practices of the past. The commercial success that usually accompanied improvement demonstrated its' validity in terms of increased production, but the prejudices of the improvers have helped to further obscure the realities of life for the majority of Scottish people in the medieval and early modern period. In the eighteenth and nineteenth centuries the mania for agricultural improvement swept away almost all of the traces of earlier farm practice in the race to replace the 'old ways' with modern, scientific methods.

The work of historians, unsurprisingly, tends to focus almost exclusively on the actions and fortunes of the great and good. This is an unfortunate, if inevitable consequence of trying to unravel the story of medieval Scotland. Any study of the Kingdom is bound to be preoccupied primarily with the leaders of men. In consequence there is a tendency to overlook the men that they led. The lives of the vast majority of medieval Scots are completely lost to us in terms of detailed biographical data of individuals. Scotland has no equivalent of the Paxton letters to shed light on the lives of the lower gentry and their servants. There is no shortage of evidence of the *existence* of the lower gentry and the peasant classes. The gentry figure in the witness lists of their lords charters, the peasants as part of the stock referred to in those charters. Concerning the gentry we can ascertain a good deal from documentary evidence, primarily charters granting feudal land tenure. The granting or confirmation of a charter tells us about the land that the recipient of the charter is to enjoy and the rights that go with it. The charter will also make clear the services that the recipient must perform in order to fulfil his contractual obligations. The rental of the property due to the superior depended on custom and the relationship between lord and vassal, rather than any concept of the real commercial value of the contract.

In a feudal society all land was in theory owned by the King. The landholder's 'property' strictly speaking was merely rented, but on perpetual, heritable leases at fixed rates. Unsurprisingly, the holders of these leases were more enthusiastic about the perpetual and heritable aspects of the contract than they were about the inherently impermanent nature of a lease. As far as they were concerned they owned their land with free and secure title so long as they performed the stipulated services appropriate to that property.

The great landowners, as royal vassals, leased their estates from the King in order to lease them out to their own vassals and dependants who in turn let them to farming tenants. At some point in this chain of contracts, the nature of the payment, '*reddendo*' changed from an 'honourable' rent of money and military service to a 'dishonourable' one of labour and produce. Once land was granted heritably, the tenant would naturally seek the erosion of any obligations due to the feudal superior, and the easiest – though in the long term most damaging – way for the superior to reward or influence his tenantry would often be to reduce those obligations. Among the gentry and aristocracy the 'rent' could be a purely symbolic payment – a pair of white gloves' or a hawk. Some of these rents are rather more astute than first glance would indicate. The fairly commonplace inclusion of a pound of pepper or cumin was effectively a hedge against inflation. Fixing payment as the weight rather than the cash value of an expensive imported product paid dividends when the value of Scottish currency as foreign exchange collapsed in the later fourteenth and fifteenth centuries.

Military service was similarly 'hedged' against inflation. The quality of equipment needed to be able to perform knight service rose steadily in the thirteenth century, but because army service was assessed in days of service rather

53. The Lothian terrain favoured raiding parties.

than a cash equivalent, the increasing cost military service in general and knight service in particular fell on those who served it rather than those who received it.

The rents of tenant farms were generally of a much more realistic economic nature than the token payments levied for estate holdings, but the cost of appropriate military kit and the regularity of military service being demanded were obviously much less. The level of labour service attached to property diminished as commutation for cash payments became commonplace through the thirteenth century. The amount of unpaid labour that an individual had to perform on a lord's estate was an indicator of a person's status in the society. The term 'class' would have been incomprehensible to medieval Scots, but they were keenly aware of status. The rising incomes of the labouring classes allowed them to reduce their level of 'unfree' obligations, leading to a rapid decline in number of people living in serfdom. Landowners were not in a hurry to give up rights of ownership in their workers nor to lose labour services incidental to land they rented out, but the convenience of operating in a money economy – even if rents were actually paid in produce – encouraged tenants to buy out their lord's rights if they felt they could make sufficiently profitable use of their time in pursuit of their own agenda to make it cost effective to either supply a hired hand to work the required days or negotiate the commutation of the labour into a cash settlement. The extent to which a tenant enjoyed freedom from labour services on his landlord's property was an indication of the extent of his personal liberty, but it is important to bear in mind that our information really relates to the property in question, not to the person who worked that property. Labour service to be provided by a tenant was part of his rent and did not necessarily imply that the tenant was not personally free. The social position of the tenant was not an issue in this. When Sir Ingram de Guines became a tenant (with three others) of property at Lamberton, he became liable for his share of the ploughing and harvest services due from that property to the manor of Ayton in just the same way that any non-noble tenant would become liable for the services attached to the property they leased. The involvement of members of the baronial class in the agricultural land market as *tenants* of farms (or of mills) as well as landlords shows that farming was seen as a potentially lucrative venture. Interest in agriculture was not limited to the peasants and the baronage. Successful burgesses bought farmland to lease not only for the profits of farming but to acquire status in the community that would allow them to join the gentry.

Not everyone fitted perfectly into our picture of the feudal pyramid. The general pattern of farm-tenants and cottars/day labourers paying rent to a lord was not absolutely universal. Proprietary farm touns existed, the toun being the property of a number of 'heritors', whose children, as the name implies, would inherit their rights in the property. The inhabitants of such a toun were not necessarily much better off than their tenant neighbours, but they obviously enjoyed security of tenure and freedom from labour services, heriots, merchets and the other trappings of feudal inferiority.

The economic advance of the lower orders of Scottish society through the thirteenth and fourteenth centuries is unmistakable and the changes in servile status that allowed farmers to expand their enterprises are both cause and product of an improving economy. The charter terms of *servi, neyf, bondi, rustici* and *nativi* may have been definitive terms to medieval Scots, but if so this information has not been recorded. The inclusion of some or all of these terms in land transactions may sometimes be little more than the preservation of legal formulae which had largely fallen into desuetude. We might be better to regard these people as sitting tenants with a security of tenure that their children would inherit rather than a completely servile class thirled to the plough. Neyfs or nativi might be thirled to the land but they were not necessarily without rights or protection. A landlord at Arbuthnott refrained from removing a serf – Gillandres the lame – when he discovered that the he was a long-standing adherent of the local bishop. The social standing of servile status is impossible to clearly ascertain. Professor Duncan has identified examples of 'free' men marrying 'villein' heiresses in order to obtain a landholding. Perhaps the land was as much 'thirled' to the villein as the villein was thirled to the land. The implication surely is that while the lord may own the land and the people who farm that land, the land is not much use to the lord without labour. If the neyfs could not prosper in their relationship with their lord they might easily desert him for another. In the climate of a declining population the 'new' lord, keen to ensure that all of his lands are in production, would be unlikely to enquire too closely into the technical 'liberty' of someone in search of a farm lease.

The lack of personal liberty did not need to be a sign of abject poverty. In 1247 a burgess of Berwick purchased a neyf for twenty Merks. This large sum is explained by the fact that the neyf in question was the 'grieve' of Prenderguest in Berwickshire and therefor a man accustomed to considerable responsibilities. As the 'manager' of the property he would have far too much opportunity to improve his financial situation at the expense of his employer/owner if he was not adequately 'looked after'. The grieve may have been a 'slave' in the strictest sense, but he was not necessarily poor.

The aristocracy may have been keen to protect their 'property rights' over other human beings, but precisely what these rights meant in practical terms may not have been particularly clear to them, let alone us. The economic developments of the twelfth and thirteenth centuries and the extension of personal liberty in the fourteenth century may have made it genuinely difficult for both landlord and tenant to be sure of their rights and responsibilities. This may have been complicated by changes in lordship. A newly-infeft lord would be unlikely to want to cause bad feeling among the tenants by demanding more of them than the previous incumbent – he would need the support of these men if his lordship was going to be successful. Perhaps more importantly, the arrival of a new lord might be a good opportunity for the tenants to play down their responsibilities to the estate, claiming traditions that their previous lord would not have recognised. Quite why servile status should have started to disappear in Scotland as early as it did is open to question, but the influx of French, English, Flemish and German merchants and artisans who settled here must have had some impact. These people did not come to Scotland to be poor; they came because of the potential rewards of operating in a rapidly modernising economy. The success stories among the immigrants would surely encourage the local Scots to aspire to the liberties and wealth of their new neighbours. Some of the newcomers came to Scotland as the

54. Agricultural Scotland. The shaded areas indicate the poorer agricultural regions.

military tenants of the king or nobles, but the majority came to exploit the growth of the Burghs.

Some quite modest landowners held their property directly from the king, and even some small tenants, though few as humble as the group of 'Kings' husbandmen' who petitioned for an improvement in their tenure status in 1305. These smallholders were seeking the same tenure rights as their counterparts in England, who had longer leases, which shows that Scottish husbandmen were aware of the different conditions in another country and were not shy of approaching the King to secure an improvement in their own status. Only a tiny proportion of smallholders were direct tenants of the King of course, but most landowners would have this sort of tenant and it is reasonable to assume that baronial tenants would be likely to want any improvement in the conditions of royal smallholders to be extended to themselves.

Below the smallest tenants there was a class of landless men who depended on labouring in other men's fields for their daily bread. This pool of labour was vital for the economy. Landless men had the most time available to perform it, but terms like 'cottar' or 'husbandman' should not be seen as strict social stratifications, day-labouring was potentially an important part of the income of smallholders as it still is in many parts of the country. Labour wages could also supplement the incomes of people who were not strictly members of the rural economy. Eyemouth in Berwickshire was founded as a trading port and fishing settlement to serve the Priory of Coldingham, but of the fish bones recovered by excavation, the vast majority seem to have been caught in the summer months. This suggests that the villagers found harvest time employment on nearby farms since the inhabitants of the village were mostly landless cottars.

Their lack of arable land is further indicated by a rental of c.1430 in which the nineteen cottar holdings are assessed rentals comprising money and fish, but no agricultural produce. Even within a small settlement like Eyemouth there was some variety in the tenure of the inhabitants. Beside the cottars there were four freeholders, presumably farmers whose products could be processed in a local mill that had not been mentioned in the previous rental of c.1300. The main 'internal' enterprises of the township were fishing and brewing, (four breweries c.1300 – surely more than enough for the inhabitants of a village with only twenty-five houses, nine of them unoccupied) but the line between farmer and tradesman was not a hard and fast distinction. If the fishermen were involved in agriculture, the freeholders could be involved in the commercial activity of the village. The trading carried out for Coldingham would have called for labour and provide opportunities. The Prior's interest in fishing was commercial. In around 1270 the Priory had three fishing boats and two other boats; smaller, but still needing four oarsmen apiece. Dried fish was an important Scottish export, but even a very large-scale enterprise would leave little trace in the landscape due to the extremely biodegradable nature of the waste products.

The rapid (by medieval standards) development of the economy in the thirteenth century changed the nature of Scottish society, but it also made Scotland an attractive proposition to an expansionist neighbour, Edward I of England. The lengthy wars of independence he engendered probably hastened the decline of servile status through the widespread disruption of the community that can be expected of any war. If we reject the proposition that medieval Scotland was an uncommonly primitive and poverty-stricken society, we should be equally careful not to exaggerate the prosperity of that community. Almost without exception, visitors to Scotland paint a pretty bleak picture of both the land and the people. A French knight who appears in John Barbour's romance 'The Bruce' describes Perth – one of the most important, largest and wealthiest of Scottish 'burghs' as a 'wrechyt hamillet' – wretched hamlet – which at the very least tells us how Barbour (who had travelled to London and to Paris) thought a foreigner might see what in Scottish terms was a rather grand place.

The prevalence of runrig tends to give us an unrealistic picture of a standard format of farming practice in medieval Scotland; the arable divided into long rigs allocated to individuals, an infield under continual cultivation which gets all the manure, outlying pastures intermittently cultivated and a head dyke to separate the two. The reality of agricultural practice was rather more diverse. The precise nature of each farm depended on its situation and local traditions and conditions. An area of good arable land might be set to less profitable pasture if the area in question was prone to military activity, because flocks and herds can obviously be moved more easily than standing crops or stored produce. The purpose of runrig may well have been to 'collectivise' labour, tools and 'plant' in the shape of draught animals, a development that is unlikely to have been uniform either in time or form so we should not be surprised at regional or local variations in agricultural activity. References to runrig are common from the fifteenth century (Professor Barrow has identified a late twelfth century righolder in 'Ballebotlia 'toun). The term 'infieldland ' first appears in a fifteenth century tack for Abirbrothy in Angus, but 'infields' were common throughout the east of Scotland. This field would receive the bulk of the manure and was sometimes referred to as 'mukkitland'. 'Mukkitland would be more or less continuously cultivated, and in marginal areas the exhaustion of the infield beyond the capacity of dung to repair the damage would lead to the abandonment of the town and the incorporation of its grazing into other farms.

If we accept that runrig was the common approach, we should remember the exceptions – desmesne farming was not generally an important feature of land use in medieval Scotland but it was not unknown. Unless the formation of rigs was going to be a major improvement in the drainage of the field there would be no reason to adopt rigs if there was no reason to divide productivity on an individual basis. And why should a cottar with perhaps as little as two or three acres subdivide his field into narrow plots given the labour involved in digging and maintaining deep furrows which would effectively reduce the size of his field?

When we consider the buildings in which people lived and worked, we again find a more sophisticated situation than we might expect. Unfortunately the most common materials used for construction – turf and wattle and daub – do not generally survive well. Roman turf fortifications have been successfully excavated, but they were massive constructions built under professional supervision, the less substantial dwellings of medieval Scottish peasants have simply dissolved due to weather erosion or almost all trace of them has disappeared under more recent

55. Regardless of war, farming had to continue.

construction. Due to the continuous occupation of farm locations, an unrepresentatively large proportion of medieval archaeology in Scotland is urban. The majority of the buildings investigated both in rural and urban settings, have been wattle and daub constructions, but there is a considerable variety in the construction styles. The nature of the materials did not mean that the houses were all hovels. The bishops of St Andrews owned a manor house at Stobo near Peebles to which they could retreat; it is fair to assume that it was reasonably comfortable. Robert I built himself a manor house at Cardross, so presumably a manor could be at least as comfortable and even perhaps as prestigious as a castle. Self-evidently it could be a fit home for a King, even one as conscious of prestige as Robert I.

On a less exalted level, a successful merchant like John Mercer or Eleanor Monkton would presumably like to enjoy the fruits of their labour. The appearance of someone's home – especially if it is his or her place of business – is an indicator of status. An Inverness burgess who had expensive plank cladding added to his house had it installed only on the wall facing the street where it could make an impression on the people of the town. An excavation at Inverness has revealed clay walls 'supported by vertical oak planks or staves', wattle and clay-daub, and plank walls set into sill-beams all contemporary and in the same location. Similar work in Aberdeen showed an equal variety of construction methods, and also some houses built on stone sill work, which suggests a certain degree of permanency. This might well be a result of increasing prosperity and a considerable amount of re-development in the fourteenth century, but may just be a reflection of local fashion. Householders in the towns built according to taste and pocket – presumably rural freeholders (at least) did the same. The short leases or 'tacks' that were typical of Scottish agriculture until the eighteenth century did not encourage improvement and development among small farmers. There was little point in investing in the property if the landlord was going to terminate the lease in order to let it at an increased rental to someone else. The length of an initial lease is not however an infallible guide to the *effective* duration of the let. If a farm was operating well enough for the landlord to feel confident of getting his rental there would be no particular reason for the tenant to move on at the end of the agreed period.

Excavation at Springwood Park, Kelso indicated sturdy cruck-built houses with stone walls to about one metre and a thatched roof to an apex of roughly three metres. Heather or turf were common roofing materials, but heather is scarce in Roxburghshire and in an area of good agricultural land straw would be more likely.

The more marginal the land, the greater reliance on beasts rather than crops, and the declining population of the fourteenth century would have made these marginal fields uneconomic in terms of return on labour. The fact that people were willing to invest such a lot of effort into poorer soil areas is indicative of the profitability of agriculture, but the reversion of these lands to pasture should remind us that marginal farmland was not *typical* farmland. Another, though unexplored, factor in the reversion to pasture or abandonment of farms in the later fourteenth century may have been the succession of 'good years' when crops were relatively heavy across much of Scotland. This would inevitably reduce the 'real' price of food with consequences for farms that were only marginally profitable in normal market conditions.

Where occupation of a medieval farm has been continuous to the present day – and this must be the vast majority – development has obviously hidden the past. This is not a completed pattern. The expanding use of very large prefabricated buildings around established farm steadings since the 1960s undoubtedly compounds the problem. Because of the rather insubstantial nature of wattle and daub construction many medieval sites probably go unrecognised as such. Enclosures and earthworks of the medieval landscape can be mistakenly associated with the outlines of prehistoric ring-houses that they happen to enclose.

While it is true that most people lived in small farm touns of wattle and daub construction there were people who did not. At least one stone-built village (Lour in Peebleshire) and one planned village (Midlem in Roxburghshire) have been identified. The discovery of two substantial 'Hall houses' at Rait and Morton would suggest a rising non-noble landowning class who can afford to invest in comfort as well as in commerce. A nucleated village at Camphill, enclosed with ditch and rampart indicates a degree of insecurity among the inhabitants, but it also suggests that they considered the effort of building these defences a worthwhile investment. That they had the resources to invest in such a project would further suggest that they were right.

One of the functions of Burgh administration was to set 'fair' prices for necessities. The most important of these products were bread and ale. The pricing or 'assize' of bread and ale effectively set the price of wheat and of barley. Oats do not seem to have been the subject of assizes save in times of dearth. The value of oats as a cash crop for landlords in east coast Scotland by early modern times has been amply demonstrated by T.C. Smout and A.S. Fenton '… hardly a family north of the Tay not shipping grain or meal either coastwise or abroad.' If the chief means of turning agricultural activity into cash lay in the cultivation of oats there are questions to be asked about productivity. The traditional Scots proverb '*Ane tae gnaw and ane tae saw and ane tae pay the laird with a'* is difficult to accept at face value. If a good return on oats was three grains for each one sown, how could

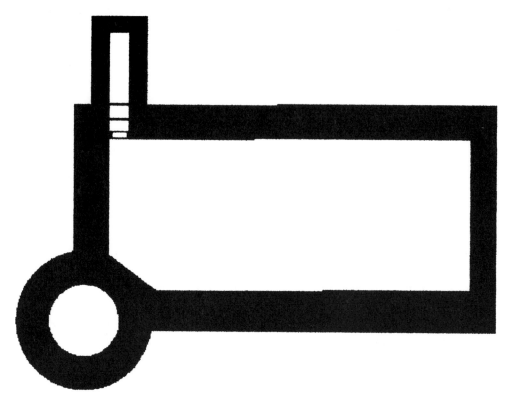

56. Rait Castle, a hall house.

farmers recover from abnormal contingencies? If the production of a farm was sufficient to provide rent, seed and sustenance and nothing more, there would be no money to make good the inevitable accumulated shortfall caused by accidental damage, unseasonable weather conditions or the passage of armies. Even the most minor crop failure would permanently undermine the economy and viability of the farm. This did of course happen from time to time. Whole settlements could go out of use but that is comparatively rare. Desertion of a site is not necessarily a product of environmental factors. The village of Mow in Berwickshire disappeared because the landowners sold off small pieces of arable land with extensive grazing rights to Kelso abbey until there was not enough to service the flocks of the villagers. Changes in the weather, soil exhaustion market forces and depopulation due to war and plague caused the abandonment of farms and villages, but chiefly from marginal lands. If a return of three for one was the norm of cereal productivity farm failure and abandonment would be much more commonplace. Possibly that level of return represents the minimum return necessary to survive and not the normal expectation of yield.

The importance of bread as opposed to oatcakes is not in itself an indication of a complete reliance on wheat. The 'mashlum' bread common throughout Scotland until the eighteenth century (at least) was made from flour of mixed grains, including barley oats and peas. The significance of peas for flour may have been overlooked. As late as 1818 (according to a report in the *Farmers Magazine* of that year) peas were 'use(d) as much as bread corn' on the Isle of Arran. This may of course be a report of a unique circumstance, but if so would surely be described as such.

It may in fact have been a common practice to sow a mixture of grains on the same plot to produce a mixed meal. Pease and barley ground together to produce 'bread meal' was still being made commercially in Perth in 1837.

Even in areas where wheat was a rarity, reliance on oats alone was not inevitable, indeed it was probably rare. The hardiness of barley and its usefulness for both bread and ale made it an attractive crop. Fenton and Smout estimated that as much as 30% of grain production went to ale, which further denies the dependence on oats monoculture that is the 'received history' picture of Scottish farming before the eighteenth century.

The poverty that early visitors to Scotland describe was very real. The vast majority of people lived what would seem to us a life of unrelieved squalor. For the poorer members of the community a poor harvest would mean a spell of serious deprivation at best and starvation at worst.

The life of the medieval farmer in Scotland was not an easy one, but the same applies to farmers all over Europe. Scottish peasants may have been poor, but perhaps no more so than their equivalents elsewhere. Their personal freedom may have been a little more developed than the condition of the lower orders in other

57. Caerlaverock Castle showing the wet moat.

parts of Christendom. The peasant's revolts of England, France and Germany have no counterparts in medieval Scotland.

Joint tenancies of farms may have been the norm, but the more successful members of the labouring classes could prosper, as we can see from the emergence of men who rent two or three farms and/or shares in farms. A tenant mentioned in the *Douglas Rental* was paying at least £8 a year in rents, a substantial amount of money at a time when the King might pay a fee of 10 Merks annually (£6 6s 8d) for the service of an expensively equipped knight and when labourers might get paid 1d a day. The bulk of Douglas tenants were obviously not operating at the same lever of business, but the majority of them were in sole tenants or joint tenant with one other person and paying rentals of between two and three pounds. Only about one in eight tenants had a rental less than one pound. The 229 tenants that figure in the Douglas Rental between them leased eighty-eight farms, which rather suggests that the one pound rentals were to single tenants. At a wage scale of 1d a day, the 240 pennies laid out to rent a farm was a substantial sum, so not everyone outside the gentry was as impoverished as we might expect from our 'received history' of the agrarian society of medieval Scotland.

8

THE NEVILLE'S CROSS CAMPAIGN

It is easy to accuse a commander who attacks and is defeated of having acted rashly. If, however, David had won his battle rather than lost it and gone into captivity for several years, he might have become a revered figure in the Scottish gallery of heroes, like his father, Robert I, and that was probably an important consideration in his decision to fight. Since his return from France in 1341, David had made some headway in establishing his authority over nobility that had enjoyed a lot of freedom from royal control. The return of the king indicated a growing confidence among the Scots, but it was also a natural progression in the policies the Scots had adopted when they sent David to France in the first place. When David landed at Inverbervie in 1341 he was still in his teens, and the magnates of Scotland would not have relinquished all of the power of the state to him until he had become more accustomed to the realities of Scottish political life than he could hope to achieve while living in France, however well-briefed he might have been by Scottish lords and clerics visiting his court at Chateau Gaillard at the mouth of the Seine.

The disruption of war had allowed magnates a much greater degree of independence from the power of the crown than had been the case in the reign of Robert I (once he had established his kingship) or of Alexander III. Any rise in the power of the aristocracy was almost inevitably at the expense of the royal authority, and in any case, David was coming to an age where he had to become more involved in the affairs of his kingdom. To fight in the cause of a child-king in exile was rather different to fighting for an adult living a comfortable life abroad. By 1341 the Scots were in the ascendant militarily, and in fact would continue to be so for some time. There were still several castles and towns held by English garrisons for Edward III, but they were no longer able to perform the vital functions of an occupying force – gathering taxes and discouraging the opposition. In a sense they were a liability. Edward III's exchequer had to find almost all of the wages and supply costs of the

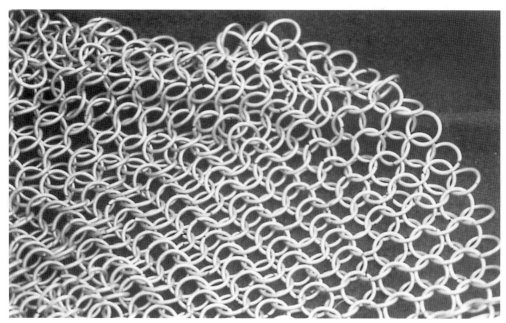

58. Detail of a chainmail hood - note that the links are butted together rather than riveted. Butted mail, being much cheaper, was probably more common than riveted mail.

59. Two layers of padded cloth armour was probably nearly as good protection as chainmail and a jack, and considerably less expensive, but cumbersome.

troops and the maintenance of the fabric of the castles. In part these costs could be met, even perhaps *had* to be met, for the sake of Edward III's regal prestige; the massive expense of his operations in Scotland would be unacceptable if there was nothing at all to show for the outlay. There was however a more tangible reason to continue to support these garrisons. The war with France, which was of much greater interest to Edward III than anything that might happen in Scotland, drew heavily on his military resources, and the Scots were allies of the French. Edward hoped that the network of strongholds that he maintained in Scotland would keep the Scots busy enough that they would be unable to make a concerted attack on the north of England while he was campaigning in France with the cream of his manpower.

Militarily, this policy probably paid for itself in the years following Edward's first French expedition. His options were kept open without demanding a full commitment to his Scottish war. The garrisons were costly, but not as costly as committing large armies to Scottish expeditions that would almost inevitably fail to force significant battle on the Scots. Even if he had had the men to fight campaigns of manoeuvre on both fronts he did not have the capacity to pay the troops: even if he could force the Scots to give battle there was no guarantee that his army would necessarily win such a battle, and the damage to his military prestige and royal authority if that army was defeated might be irreparable. If the Scots could be brought to battle and defeated, Edward's fortunes might not be improved to any great extent. Despite the vast sums spent on operations in Scotland and despite the outstanding battlefield triumph of Halidon Hill not a great deal had been achieved in terms of furthering the interests of England, and people resented the heavy taxation that was necessary to fund a war of conquest that was manifestly failing to conquer.

The growing success of the Scots after the battle of Culblean was certainly a factor in encouraging them to carry the conflict into England, but there were a number of political considerations that David could not afford to ignore. The lords that had been in the forefront of the campaigns to remove English garrisons since Halidon Hill in 1333, had been fighting in King David's cause, and some of them – such as William Douglas and John Randolph, Earl of Moray – had acquired great status for their martial exploits against the English. If David were to be truly King he would have to achieve a similar status. A baron or magnate could enhance their reputation through the successful conduct of several minor actions, but if David wanted to establish his authority through his military activity he could most effectively do so through inflicting a major defeat on his enemy in a large-scale engagement.

In October 1346 David had a number of reasons to believe that a good opportunity had arisen for him to win a battle that would bring him personal prestige at home and credibility with his ally, France, whose support and hospitality he had enjoyed for many years. A battlefield success in the north of England rather than in Scotland might even help to wring recognition of his kingship from Edward III, who had recognised Edward Balliol as king of Scots since 1332. More realistically, a Scottish victory might well demoralise the few remaining English/Balliol garrisons, thus extending David's kingship without conducting lengthy sieges which might not be concluded successfully and which would very probably result in substantial damage to the castles themselves. Since the Scots had by now abandoned their policy of slighting (demolishing, or at least rendering indefensible) the castles they captured. The fact that the Scots could now hope to maintain those castles and provide garrisons for them was an indicator in itself of their growing confidence.

David was not completely devoid of military experience. He had participated in at least two operations in England and had served the king of France in Flanders in 1340. In July 1346 he had participated in a campaign led by the Earl of Moray, which had brought destruction to the north-west of England but no tangible military results. No English army appeared to obstruct the Scots and they returned home without loss. Travelling incognito was a romantic and chivalrous thing to do, but it had a practical application. If the force travelled under David's banner and was confronted by an English force too strong to be opposed, there might be some damage to the prestige of the young king. If they travelled under the banner of the Earl of Moray they could withdraw without embarrassment. There was the world of difference in terms of status between the Earl of Moray raiding into England and the king of Scots formally setting out to war.

David was aware of the practical political importance of military success as well as being an enthusiast for chivalry. The army he took to England must have fallen well short of the some of figures offered by contemporary writers, but Scottish and English documents are agreed that it was a very large army indeed.

The consistency of estimates of Scottish men-at-arms deserves to be taken seriously. The suggestion of 2000 men-at-arms would be a huge turnout of the Scottish nobility

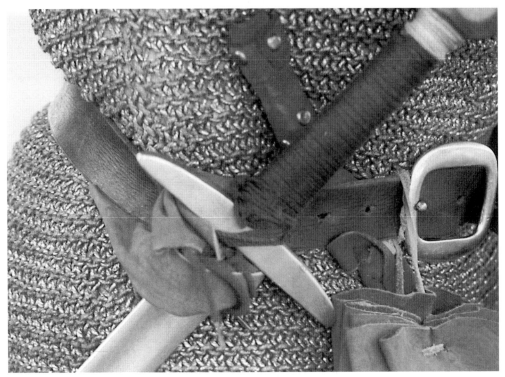

60. Scabbards were cumbersome and seldom carried into battle. This form of arrangement was much more practical.

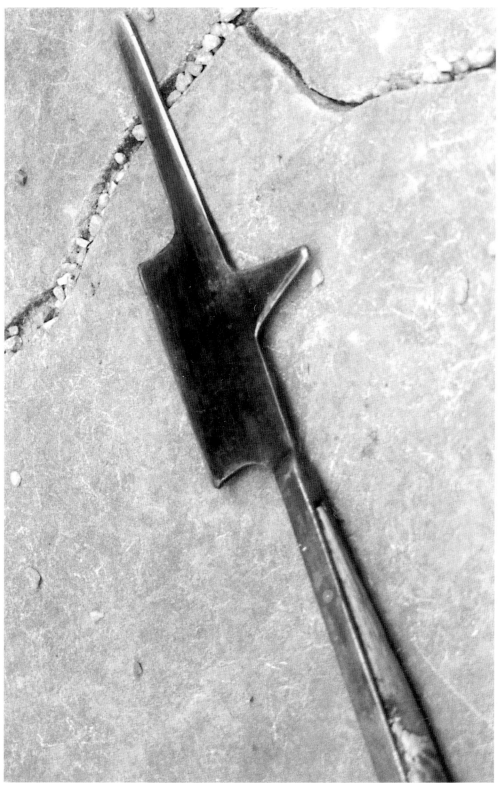

61. A heavy polearm was much more effective than a sword.

and gentry, but not an impossible one. The equally consistent estimates of 20,000 lightly armoured soldiers and a further mass of unarmoured 'hangers on' is much less credible. In the seventeenth century, with a larger population and an immensely more sophisticated and intensive administration Scotland raised – and to a considerable extent sustained recruiting and logistical maintenance for – an army of 20,000, recruited from a larger population and on a wider geographical base than David's. If his spearmen and archers comprised as much as 10 or 12, 000 that would be a very impressive host for a Scottish king. Robert I had raised an army of perhaps 6000 to 8000 in 1314, and while it is true that David could recruit more successfully in Lothian and the borders than his father could, he did not have the same support from the west that his father had enjoyed through his alliance with Angus Og. The Lord of the Isles had been a reliable ally to Robert I and had supplied him with troops for campaigns all over Scotland, Ireland and the north of England. Angus Og's successor, John, had done his utmost to remain aloof from the struggles of the Bruce and Balliol parties, he had even been named as an ally of Edward III at one point, and his return to the Bruce party was self-evidently a matter of political expediency rather than heart-felt sympathy for the king. His primary interest was the continuing independence of his family in the Western Isles. As long as the Scottish kingship was in contention and the position of the Scottish king weak, the Lord of the Isles could protect his very considerable independence and possibly extend his lordship in mainland areas of western Scotland such as Kintyre and Knapdale.

Even if we accept the estimates of the Scottish army strength from chronicle accounts there are questions to be asked about the administrative and tactical format of such a massive force. The division of an army something in excess of 20,000 into just three formations seems less than practical. If the divisions were of equal strength, each would comprise about 7000 men, moving around the field as single entities. The command system and drill standards necessary to bring that about would have to be massively sophisticated, intensively rehearsed and perfectly executed to enable such a unit to perform even the simplest evolutions effectively let alone co-ordinate its manoeuvres with two other formations. Even assuming that such a thing is possible at all; it was certainly beyond the capacities of medieval Scottish armies. It is true that a Roman Legion had a theoretical ration strength of about 6000, but in reality a legion would seldom comprise more than about two-thirds that figure. Marshalling a Roman army was a complicated business carried out by trained professional officers and junior leaders commanding regular career soldiers.

If we make the rather arbitrary assumption that King David's army was only half of the size given by Bower – and ignoring the horde of camp followers – each division of David's army would be still be over 3000 strong, perhaps twice the size of the schiltroms at Bannockburn and a rather bigger body of people than the complete population of most Scottish towns. Certainly the formations were big enough to be unable to negotiate the 'dykes and ditches' of the battlefield without becoming disrupted and David found himself in a 'richt annoyus place' unable to manoeuvre, but among the small farm enclosures on a slope bounded by the steep ravine of the river Brownie on one side and the environs of the city of Durham on the other a line formation (as opposed to a column) would not have to be very big before it found its scope for manoeuvre sharply limited.

The campaign of 1346 was David's first, and of course last, attempt to raise a large 'national' force, and in the interests of keeping on the right side of the king if nothing else recruiting is likely to have been quite successful. The Scots had been having the best of the war for some time, and the prospect of looting Cumbria and Northumberland would have been a considerable incentive to enlistment. The size of his army suggests that David was prepared to accept or offer battle should the opportunity present itself. If, as is often suggested, the campaign was intended primarily as a punitive raid to distract Edward III's attention from his war in France then a much smaller, mobile force like the Scottish army of the 1327 Weardale campaign would have been more appropriate. David's own experience would have told him so if the people around him did not. The involvement of the magnates who had been directing the war (at least) until David's return to Scotland in 1341 in the campaign has not been considered as a factor encouraging David to fight. No doubt Bower is right in telling us that David took the advice of young men of no experience, but the 'old hands' were present as well and only Douglas, having fulfilled his own 'war aims' seems to have advised anything other than an advance into England. Douglas however had rather different priorities to the king, and by capturing the peel at Liddesdale and collecting booty he had fulfilled those priorities to his own entire satisfaction. David 's prestige would not be enhanced by the brief incursion into England of a large army that did not seek battle or refused it if offered. If an English army were to approach David's force it would be very difficult for him *not* to fight without damage to his reputation. The conduct of the Scots in the days immediately before the battle is a further indication of their goals. The ransom of

62. Arbour House Farm. The Scottish army deployed for battle in this area.

the town and county of Durham may have been attractive to David, but not worth the risk of a general engagement. Several communities in the north of England had already made ransom agreements with the invaders, so David was probably not particularly strapped for funds. If David could defeat the English in battle, Durham would be his for the taking anyway. If he could defeat the English without seriously damaging his own force he could even consider moving further south since it would be some time before a new army could be raised against him.

Tactically, David was unlikely to get another opportunity to engage on such potentially advantageous terms. His army was larger than his enemy's, it had been successful to date and he believed – so Bower and Fordoun tell us – that the bulk of English fighting strength was in France. If David was looking for a fight, and it is difficult to believe otherwise, he was looking for one like the battle of Myton in 1319, a sharp victory in the enemy's country. If he outnumbered his enemy by a factor of 2:1 then the pressure on him to exploit the advantage would have been immense. If he did not fight he would have to retire in the face of an inferior enemy and probably be forced to abandon loot and equipment. The damage to his authority would be huge, whereas the reputations of his magnates, even if they had been instrumental in persuading him to retire to Scotland, would be unimpaired and David would continue to reign in their shadows. He might never be able to exert his authority over them.

It is possible that he did not outnumber his enemy dramatically but that he hoped he would be able to face them down without giving battle. It was not unknown for large field armies to approach one another but not fight. A show of strength, a challenge that the English did not accept would suit David almost as well as victory in battle. If he could lead his army home unscathed and laden with the wealth of northern England, his kingship would be affirmed by military success, his enemy, Edward, would be undermined and he would have struck a blow, however minor, for his ally, France.

The assumption that the English were ill prepared does not withstand examination. Edward had made arrangements for the defence of northern England before his departure for France, entrusting reliable, experienced local magnates with responsibility for raising troops and conducting operations in the event of Scottish attacks. There may have been an expectation among the English officers that the Scots would join in an Anglo-French truce, which was being negotiated in the wake of the spectacular English victory at Crecy. Certainly the reactions of the English commanders was not immediate, but they were not exactly taken by surprise. A Scottish attack in support of the French war effort had been expected for some time and there was a system in place to raise an army sufficient to counter a Scottish intervention south of the Tweed. The size of that army is open to question. Dr. Prestwich suggests a total of 1000 men-at-arms from magnatial and baronial retinues, 3000 archers from Yorkshire and nearly 1000 more from Lancashire, the last two figures coming from pay roll information. He offers a total English field strength of 1000 men at arms and 5000 infantry, which would infer that only 1000 men could be raised from Northumberland, Cumbria, Westmoreland, Norhamshire, the city and county of Durham and the following of Edward Balliol, said to have been present with more than 100 men-at-arms. It is of course quite possible, even likely, that the contribution of these communities was smaller than might normally have been expected, but even so, a total of 1000 men from such a large swathe of northern England at a time of obvious national danger seems to be an improbably low figure.

Although it is the recognised tradition of chronicle accounts to exaggerate enormously the sizes of armies, there is a compelling consistency in the estimates of men-at-arms. The figure of 800 men-at-arms offered by the *Anonimalle Chronicle* seems unusually realistic for a chronicle account. More unusually there is a similar consistency in the numbers given for the infantry. Several sources give a figure of 9000 or 10,000 – again, a realistic sounding figure given that the English were as prepared as the Scots to offer or accept battle. If the English army had not been big enough to give its commanders the confidence to offer battle there would not have been a battle at all. Edward III might be angry if the Scots mounted a successful operation in the north of his country, but it had happened before and would probably happen again. On the other hand if an English army were to be destroyed in battle, the foreign and domestic political advantage and prestige that he had gained at Crecy would be lost. Edward's lieutenants did not lightly decide to seek an engagement, they did so with confidence In the fourteenth century as in any other period, commanders chose the combat option in circumstances that they felt favoured themselves more than their enemy. They did not fight because they believed that they *could* win, but in the belief that they *would*. A battle is always a risk of course, but they obviously thought that the risk was justified by the situation and outweighed by the potential for victory. The precedence of the English commanders in their region would be confirmed, possibly improved, by a grateful monarch, their martial reputations would be enhanced and there might be financial rewards, either from the crown or in the form of ransoms – possibly both – if they could secure a victory that would force the Scots to retire from northern England. Who was in overall tactical command of the English army is unclear. William de la Zouche, Archbishop of York and William de Norwell, Bishop of Carlisle shared responsibility with four northern lords – Percy, Neville, Scrope and Mauley – and two Scots, Edward Balliol and the titular Earl of Angus. They may have been jointly responsible for the administration and implementation of strategic issues, but shared tactical command is difficult even with the most sophisticated means of communication. Edward III was surely far too competent a ruler to permit such a dangerous situation to arise. The members of the English command structure with the widest experience of warfare were Percy and Edward Balliol. Even though Balliol was a trusted officer of Edward III's military administration, it might have been considered politically inappropriate for a Scot to be in command of an English army from an English point of view, and indeed unwise for Balliol to be seen as the commander of an English army that would (they hoped) inflict a defeat on the Scots. Edward Balliol may not have harboured much hope of ever attaining the Scottish throne by this time, but there would be even less chance of him realising his ambition if he was seen as an enemy of Scottish national feeling as opposed to the enemy of David II.

Both sides then, appear to have been willing to come to battle in general terms, and both were willing to fight on the moorland west of Durham and south of the Bearpark – an area of enclosed woodland where the Scots had made their camp.

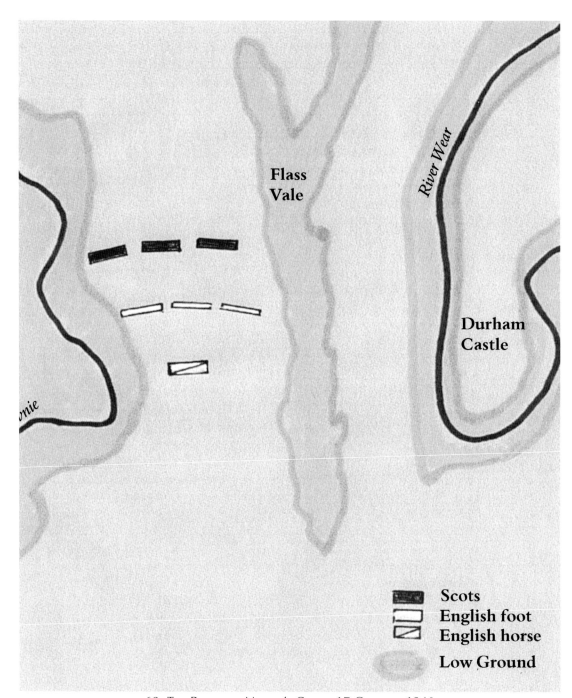

Flass
Vale

River Wear

Durham
Castle

nie

Scots
English foot
English horse

Low Ground

63. The Battle of Neville's Cross, 17 October 1346

Surprised by the approach of an unexpected English army, David II decided that attack was his best option. His army advanced toward the English across a narrow plateau between the Flass Vale and the River Brownie, approximately one mile from the city of Durham. The Scottish formations were badly disrupted by dykes and hedges and were unable to properly co-ordinate their actions. The battle largely consisted of a melee of spearmen and men at arms, sufficiently lengthy that, according to one contemporary commentator, the armies drew back from one another twice to recover their breath before returning to the fight. Author illustration.

Douglas had encountered the advance elements of the English army as he led a foraging expedition and had been forced to retire hurriedly, but the Scottish army could hardly be said to have been surprised in a grand tactical sense. It is difficult to accept any suggestion that David was not prepared to fight a major action. Douglas had been surprised by an advance party, but the Scots still had plenty of time to prepare for battle or to retreat according to David's wishes. The English may have been determined to offer battle, but David was not absolutely obliged to accept it. There are no strikingly obvious tactical issues preventing his withdrawal other than the likelihood of having to abandon his plunder and the damage that might accrue to his kingly prestige if he were to refuse battle with an army not led by the king of England and not of overwhelming superiority.

The English started the main engagement by advancing a party of archers, 500 strong according to the *Meaux Chronicle*, in an effort to goad the Scots into advancing. David refused to allow a cavalry attack to disperse these archers despite the pleas and (very chivalrous) example of Sir John Graham, Earl of Menteith who wanted to lead that attack sufficiently keenly that he charged the enemy on his own. Refraining from attacking may have been the better tactical option, since the archers do not seem to have achieved the awesome 'hailstorm' effect demonstrated by their counterparts at Crecy. David's defeat does not necessarily invalidate his refusal to engage a part of his force at a given moment. Possibly he was deliberately reserving the (probably rather limited) cavalry element of the army for a different operational task, such as the pursuit of the English army if he was successful in battle. This brings into question the nature of the troops available to the English. The record may describe the men as archers, but if there were 4000 longbowmen in the English army, surely the nature of the battle would reflect that? The troops may be described as 'archers' out of convenience or ignorance, but possibly they were enlisted on the promise of being *paid* at a preferred rate, as archers rather than 'footmen' either for convenience or as an incentive to enlist since archers enjoyed a better rate of pay than other infantry. The great longbow victories of Crecy before Neville's Cross and Poitiers and Agincourt afterwards have unreasonably influenced most historians in their appreciation of medieval battle. The clear deployment lines of a longbow battle on a map makes an attractive and convincing picture, which it is all too tempting to apply to other actions.

All the accounts of the battle emphasise its lengthy duration, describing it as a long hard slog at close quarters. The archers perform an important function, but it is the men-at-arms and the spearmen that win the day. To some extent this is of course reflects social values. The brave exploits of the gentry were more likely to be discussed in greater detail by contemporary writers if only because the writer (and the reader) knew whom they were talking about. It was in any case a reasonable interpretation of battle for a civilian to make. The men-at-arms could obviously go to battle without the support of the archers, their mobility allowing them to evade encounters with combined arms opponents, but the archers would be impossibly vulnerable without the men-at-arms to defend them when the enemy came to close quarters.

The precise location of the engagements cannot be positively identified, however the general consensus of opinion is that the English left flank rested near the gorge of the river Brownie, with the rest of the army, like the Scots in three divisions, lying in the vicinity of Neville's Cross itself, facing roughly north. Presumably both sides were taking advantage of the terrain to refuse one flank. Whether it was the Scots or the English that initiated the close combat phases of the action, it was not an easily or quickly achieved victory; the battle was waged, allegedly, for some hours before the Scots were defeated. Different writers tell us that the battle was not a continuous action. The Scots are subjected to 'two whirlwind attacks', the English are forced to retire and reform, the two armies rest and then re-join battle by agreement.

If David was trying to execute an attack *en echelon* in the hope of turning the open flank of his enemy. these statements might all refer to the same two events viewed from different locations by people with a limited insight to the conduct of battle The clash of Moray's division with the English, followed by a short lull before the engagement of David's division followed by another lull before the retreat of the Stewart's force. Most of the participants, and probably all of the commentators, would never have seen a large battle before, and it would be extremely difficult, even for an experienced combatants or bystander to identify or analyse the intentions of either army, even once the battle was completely developed, without an unnaturally favourable point of observation.

The withdrawal of the third Scottish formation under the Steward drew criticism at the time which has been repeated by Scottish historians ever since. It is true that the Steward was a political enemy of David II and would have had good reasons of his own to abandon his King to capture, but if his troops had observed the destruction of the first two divisions he may have found it impossible to persuade them to join battle in support of a defeated force. Since the Scots had already been beaten in two fights there would have been little point in reinforcing failure. An even longer casualty list would not have been a useful contribution to the day. If the Steward led a formation of lightly armed/armoured men whose intended role on the battlefield was to provide a 'final push' once the armies were both heavily engaged, his retreat was forced on him by the turn of events. If the two stronger Scottish formations could not defeat their opponents the Steward could not realistically hope to make much impression on the situation by committing his own division. If he had no effective response to make to English archery there was no future in standing his ground. If a force cannot either advance or maintain its position, self-evidently it must retreat. Finally, if David had been killed or captured, the Steward's primary duty as heir presumptive and the obvious, almost inevitable, choice as Guardian or regent, was to salvage whatever forces he could from the battlefield and return home to take part in the government of the country rather than commit more resources to a lost fight.

On the other hand, the Steward could be accused of leaving the battle at a critical juncture and thereby allowing the remaining Scots to be defeated in detail, and the king captured. The heir to the throne had failed to support his king in battle, which is scarcely a convincing demonstration of loyalty. The Steward may or may not have acted in the best interests of his country, but he had done nothing to endear himself to his king.

Large general engagements were rare events in Anglo-Scottish wars. The previous one to Neville's Cross had been thirteen years before, and had been the business of a contract army recruited from all over Edward IIIs domains. The Neville's cross

64. Flass Vale, on the left flank of David II's army at Neville's Cross.

army was a product of the traditional army service obligations of the communities of northern England. The proportion of men in the English army who had witnessed a major battle was small, but there were a few. Sir John Neville had served at the battle of Crecy just a few weeks before and the Stewart had participated in the battle of Halidon Hill in July 1333. Both sides had plenty of combat experience, but in small actions, raids and stormings, not in major open field battles. The record of the Scots in large battles suggests that they were wise to avoid having them more often. Ironically, David's capture would be a contributory factor in his eventually achieving his war aims. He was only a valuable prisoner to Edward if Edward recognised him as King of Scots, effectively undermining the claims of David's rival for the throne, Edward Balliol.

The defeat and capture of David II did not bring the war to a close, though perhaps fleetingly Edward Balliol may have been able to convince himself that there was light at the end of the tunnel. There was no immediate prospect of being able to take advantage of the victory at Durham because he had no army with which to exploit his good fortune. The troops who had fought at Neville's Cross had homes to go to and were in no hurry to go anywhere else. Some of them may not even have hung about long enough to get paid for their efforts. Edward Balliol had to wait until May 1347 before he could set out in search of kingship. The army he had collected was paid for by Edward III, but it scarcely represented the full power of the English state. Balliol's force amounted to something over 3000 men; it was more than strong enough to meet any force that the Scots might gather against him. Any two or three Scottish earls might be able to raise that many men between them, but only a small proportion of those men would be comparable in equipment or training to the bulk of the men in Balliol's army. Superficially, Balliol's campaign was a runaway success. Towns and castles throughout southern Scotland were surrendered to him almost as quickly as he could approach them. Crucially, however, the three most important strongholds, Edinburgh, Stirling and Dunbar were all retained by the Scots. This posed two military problems for Balliol. Dunbar castle threatened his landward communications with Berwick and Newcastle, Edinburgh castle threatened any administration he set up in Lothian and denied him the full benefit of Scotland's most important town and Stirling castle denied him the lowest crossing of the river Forth thereby compromising any future expedition towards Perth. The other problem was one of dwindling manpower. Most, if not all, of the castles and towns that had surrendered would have had to have some level of Balliol presence installed to ensure continuing loyalty. Some of them would need to be provided with complete garrisons. Since he had started his campaign with an army of only 3000 in the first place, depletion would be rapid, but he could not hope to impose his administration without a network of strong places guarded by armed men. Any progress made in his cause was short-lived, and by 1354 the Scots had recovered virtually everything that had been lost after Neville's Cross with the exceptions of Roxburgh and Berwick.

If either of the Edwards had high hopes after the battle of Neville's Cross they came to nothing. Edward III realised that there was no value to having the Scottish king as his prisoner unless he recognised that kingship himself, but he also discovered that although the Scots would be willing to pay a price for the liberty of their king, there was a limit. They would be prepared to discuss money, but not politics, with England. Edward hoped to achieve from David Bruce the thing that Edward Balliol was willing but unable to give. Regal suzerainty over the kings of Scotland. David himself plied up and down from London to Berwick, ostensibly helping to further negotiations whereby he would be released, possibly with little or no ransom, on the understanding that one of Edward III's sons, or even possibly Edward himself would inherit David's crown should he die without an heir. Whether or not David himself took these negotiations seriously is highly questionable, but was unimportant at the time, since the Scottish parliament would not accept any thing of the kind. If they could not free their king, they made it clear that they were quite happy to make themselves a new one, pending which, they were willing to fight in the meantime if need be.

To some extent a lull in hostilities was brought about by a natural disaster. The great plagues of the fourteenth century had less apparent impact on Scotland than on other countries, a product perhaps of a cooler climate and a lower population density, but even if Scotland was not too badly affected, France and England each lost a third or more of their people. This presented Edward III with problems – it might be more difficult to recruit and the commissioners of array would not be able to be as particular about the men they chose – but it was also an opportunity. His enemy in France was afflicted with the same problem. If Edward could find the men to pursue his French ambitions he would be able to impose his lordship more easily if the communities he captured had no energy to spare to resist him. The potential gain from advancing his own interests in France greatly outweighed the desirability of imposing Edward Balliol's kingship in Scotland.

The Scottish front was left to the devices of Edward Balliol and north of England lords while Edward devoted himself to France until 1355. In an effort to revive the Scottish war and distract Edward III, the French King, John, sent one of his knights, Eugene de Garencieres, with a party of men at arms and a large sum of money. The money was to be used to persuade Scottish magnates to break the limitations of the truce by raiding into the north of England, the men-at-arms were there to show the commitment of the French to providing armed support in time of war. They were more than a token presence. Throughout the Anglo-Scottish wars of the fourteenth century, most combat operations were conducted by very small groups of men, most of them serving for only very short periods. Even a body of fifty men, equipped to the very highest standard and available indefinitely could be a very welcome boost for the Scots. The Scots could call upon their own men-at-arms of course, but there were not too many of them, and they would only each be due forty days knight service and forty days common army service.

The French knights did not have to wait long to see action. English raids on the lands of the Earl of March provoked a retaliation by the forces of March and Douglas. The main part of their army remained hidden on the Scottish side of the Tweed while a force of 400 (according to *Scalacronica* author Sir Thomas Grey who was taken prisoner by the Scots during this engagement) under the command of Sir William Ramsay. Ramsay led his men on a punitive raid into Norhamshire, where he burned and plundered in the traditional manner. On the approach of an English force under Sir Thomas, Ramsay made a feigned retreat to draw his enemy toward him, and turned on him at Nisbet. The force under Ramsay probably comprised the mounted men-at-arms elements of Douglas and March's army with the French knights of de Garencieres.

A few weeks afterwards there was another blow to Edward's power in Scotland. The Earl of Angus made a water borne attack on Berwick. He landed his troops in the night, and at dawn they made a sudden assault with ladders in the Cowgate area of the town. The inhabitants soon gave up the struggle, but the Scots could not manage to take the castle. Preoccupied as he was with affairs in France, Edward could not ignore the fall of Berwick. Gathering an army he made for the border, but not to achieve another victory like Halidon Hill. Even if the castle had fallen to Angus' assault it would have been foolhardy for the Scots to attempt to hold the town in the face of the army that Edward *would* undoubtedly assemble if he had to. With the castle in English hands any prospect of defending Berwick was out of the question, so the Scots withdrew from the town and the burgesses surrendered on terms.

Having brought an army to Scotland, Edward had to do something with it. The expense in raising such a force could not be justified by the surrender of one town, and Edward had to indicate to the Scots that he was not prepared to give up Berwick, and that attacks on it have terrifying repercussions. He would lead his army on a campaign of destruction that would become known as 'the burnt candlemass', but while he was still at Roxburgh, he was approached by Edward Balliol. No longer young and with little prospect of ever establishing himself as king, Edward Balliol had had enough. Denigrating the Scots for not joining his cause, or if they did, not being loyal to it, he resigned his claim to the Scottish throne to Edward III. Balliol had been a paid officer of Edward III for several years, nominally at least for a wage of thirty shillings a day in peacetime and fifty shillings a day in wartime. These were tidy sums, but out of them Balliol had to maintain troops and some semblance of a royal household. Pension arrangements were made for Balliol in light of his quitclaim of the crown to Edward III and he retired to a life of leisure.

Unable to persuade the Scottish parliament to accept any infringement of sovereignty Edward made the best of a bad job. David was freed on the seventh of October 1357 for a ransom of 100,000 Merks and a truce for ten years. The Scots had not procured confirmation of the treaty of 1328. Edward never accepted that he had no feudal right in Scotland, on the other hand, he had proved incapable of enforcing his will whether he had rights or not. Although there would continue to be frequent states of war between England and Scotland, the independence of Scotland was never really an issue after the truce/ransom arrangements of 1357. However Edward might have presented the conflict in the diplomatic arena, there had never really been much question that this was a war about Scottish independence from England, and only incidentally a Scottish civil war between the Bruce and Balliol parties. The war ended in a truce, but the Scots had won.

PRIMARY AND
SECONDARY SOURCES

Not only is there a wide range of primary source materiel in existence, most of it is reasonably available in printed form. To some degree chronicle records need to be taken with a modest pinch of salt, particularly in any question of the number of soldiers in an army. One of the difficulties of using chronicle materiel is the validity of translation, especially if the chronicle was written in Latin – Bower's *Scotichronicon*, or in French – Thomas Grey's *Scalacronica*. The translations are perfectly sound in themselves, but both writers and translators tend to be rather lax about the application of military terms. One exception among the writers is Thomas Grey himself. The Lanercost chronicler lived close to the wars, but Thomas Grey and his father served in them. The practice of Anglo-Scottish war was part and parcel of Grey's life. His account treads a line between patriotically supporting the policy decisions of his king but still providing a valid picture of the political situation. Edward Balliol is consistently described as the king of Scotland, but his forces are 'the English' and his opponents are always described as 'the Scots'. Grey undoubtedly tries to give a clear picture of military practice, but the picture is blurred by 700 years and the haphazard approach to military terms and expressions by translators, which is compounded by the fact that we do not necessarily know for sure exactly what those terms meant to Thomas Grey. Civilian writers in his own time may have used the same terms, but were they really aware of what the term meant to a soldier? Because of his close proximity to the Scots in peacetime – he was a Northumbrian – and his active war service, Grey was perfectly familiar with the Scots. He felt no need to discuss their iniquities the way that the Lanercost Chronicler did.

Chronicle accounts from either side are, as one might expect, far from neutral. The Scottish chroniclers, Fordoun, Wyntoun and Bower are all staunchly nationalistic, as are the English writers of the Walsingham and Bridlington chronicles, but comparison does allow a modicum of reading between the lines. Bower's Scoticronicon is available in a recent translation by Dr D.E.R. Watt and is the only Scottish chronicle to offer anything like as much military information as Grey's *Scalacronica*.

Very little indeed is available in the way of Scottish government record, which is hardly surprising given the various disasters incurred by Scottish governments from the end of the thirteenth century. English government record however is liberally studded with materiel relevant to Scotland. We may not be able to tell a great deal about the forces of the Scots, but we have a wealth of information concerning their opponents. A superb example of what can be extrapolated from English exchequer and wardrobe accounts can be found in the appendices dealing with the strengths of English and Irish army contingents in Professor Nicholson's *Edward III and the Scots*.

There is a great deal of secondary source material for the first Scottish war of independence, much of which was produced in the wake of the film *Braveheart* and should be treated with great caution, but there is very little devoted solely to the second war. Since the Scots in the fourteenth century were largely fighting to preserve the form of administration they were accustomed to living under in the thirteenth century, it is necessary to examine the practices of Scottish government under Alexander III to develop an understanding. Professor Duncan's *Scotland, the Making of the Kingdom* is indispensable for those who wish to achieve a more complete picture of the nuts and bolts of medieval Scottish society in the thirteenth century and Professor Nicholson's *Scotland in the Later Middle Ages* is an invaluable study of the fourteenth century. The importance of lordship is impossible to exaggerate, and Dr Michael Brown's *The Black Douglases* is an enlightening examination of the implications of lordship for one of the most prominent families in Scotland. The social mores of knighthood influenced the men who made decisions, Professor Keene's *Chivalry* is surely the definitive work on the topic.

The English perspective is catered for by Dr. Prestwich's *The Three Edwards* among others. Not surprisingly, English military historians do tend to be more interested in Edward III's war with France than in his war with Scotland, but there is an excellent volume on the campaign of 1346, *The Battle of Neville's Cross* (Prestwich & Rollason, Eds.). For an accessible general history of England in this period readers will not go far wrong with Dr McKisack's *The Fourteenth Century* in the Oxford History of England series.

There are several colourful volumes about the arms and armour of this period, many of which are excellent, but the examples of equipment illustrated tend to be of the very best quality rather than run of the mill kit that might be worn by the rank and file. Partly this is because examples of any historical artefacts are likely to be those that were best made in the first place. Quality usually costs money and people are more inclined to value things that cost more. Much of the kit used by medieval soldiers was made of easily biodegradable materials – leather, cloth, wood – and has simply rotted away. Fortunately a good deal of evidence survives about the construction and appearance of such equipment and various enthusiasts have gone to great pains to re-create the arms and armour of the fourteenth century. The photographs of re-enactment groups used in this book have been chosen specifically to show the range of equipment used by all ranks of society. I am particularly grateful for the unstinting help of the Gaddgedlar group of medieval re-enactors, who can be contacted at www.gaddgedlar.com, and also thanks to the Carrick Eight Hundred.

FURTHER READING

PRIMARY SOURCES

Bain, J., *Calendar of Documents Relating to Scotland.*
Maitland Club, *Chronicon de Lanercost.*
Rothwell, J. (Ed.), *Chronicle of Walter of Guisborough, The.*

SECONDARY SOURCES

Bain, J., *The Edwards in Scotland, 1296-1377.*
Balfour Paul, J. (Ed.), *The Scots Peerage.*
Barron, E., *The Scottish War of Independence.*
Barrow, G.W.S., *Robert Bruce.*
Barrow, G.W.S. (Ed.), *The Kingdom of The Scots.*
Bloch, M., *Feudal Society.*
Boardman, S., *The Early Stewart Kings, Robert II and Robert III.*
Broun, Finlay & Lynch, (Eds.), *Image and Identity.*
Brown, M., *The Black Douglases.*
Contamine, P., *War in the Middle Ages.*
Cowan, E. & Macdonald, R.A. (Eds.), *Alba, Celtic Scotland in the Medieval Era.*
Cruden, S., *The Scottish Castle.*

Denholm-Young, N. (Ed.), *Vita Edwardi Secundi.*

Duncan, A.A.M., *Scotland, the Making of a Nation.*

Franklin, T.B., *A History of Scottish Farming.*

Funcken, L. & F., *Le Costume, L'Armure et les Armes au Temps de la Chevalerie.*

Gies, J. & F., *Life in a Medieval Castle.*

Grant, A., *Independence and Nationhood.*

Grant & Stringer, K. (Eds.), *Medieval Scotland.*

Hales, J.R., *Europe in the Late Middle Ages.*

Keen, M., *Chivalry.*

Lynch, Spearman & Stell, (Eds.), *The Scottish Medieval Town.*

MacKenzie, W.M., *The Scottish Burghs.*

MacNamee, C., *The Wars of the Bruces.*

MacNeill and McQueen, (Eds.), *Atlas of Scottish History to 1707.*

Mason, R. (Ed.), *Scotland and England 1286-1815.*

Menzies, G. (Ed.), *The Scottish Nation.*

Nicholson, R., *Edward III and the Scots.*

----   *Scotland the later Middle Ages.*

Prestwich, M., *The Three Edwards.*

Reid, N. (Ed.), *Scotland in the Reign of Alexander III.*

Rogers, C., *Social Life in Scotland from Early to Recent Times.*

Rollason & Prestwich, (Eds.), *The Battle of Neville's Cross 1346.*

Simpson, G.G. (Ed.), *Scotland and the Low Countries.*

Stringer, K. (Ed.), *Essays on the Nobility of Medieval Scotland.*

Sumption, J., *The Hundred Years War.*

Traquair, P., *Freedom's Sword.*

Watson, F., *Under the Hammer.*

LIST OF ILLUSTRATIONS

Colour Section

All castle plans are after Stuart Cruden. Sketches and photographs
        are copyright of the author unless otherwise stated.

INDEX

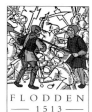

Flodden 1513
Niall Barr
'enthralling... reads as thrillingly as a novel.' *The Scots Magazine*
'an engrossing account of the battle... exemplary.' *BBC History Magazine*
'the first modern analysis... a very readable account.' *Historic Scotland*
'a very considerable achievement... fascinating and convincing.' *Military Illustrated*
160pp 65 illus. Paperback
£14.99/$32.50   ISBN 0 7524 1792 4

The Stewarts
Kings & Queens of Scotland 1371 - 1625
The accessible illustrated history of the Stewart royal family, kings and queens of the Scots from Robert II Stewart (1371-90) to James VI Stewart (1567-1625) the last Stewart monarch to really know and understand the Scots.
128pp 120 illus. Paperback
£10.99/$16.99   ISBN 0 7524 2324 X

Bloodfeud
The Stewarts & Gordons at War in the Age of Mary Queen of Scots
Harry Potter
The story of a bloody feud between warring Scottish families in the sixteenth century.
368pp 25 illus. Paperback
£17.99/$23.99   ISBN 0 7524 2330 4

Scotland
A History 8000 B.C. - 2000 A.D.
Fiona Watson
A *Scotsman* Bestseller
'Lavishly illustrated throughout, its trenchant views, surprising revelations and evocative descriptions will entrance all who care about Scotland.' *BBC History Magazine*
A comprehensive history of a proud nation written by Scotland's answer to Simon Schama, Fiona Watson, historian and presenter of BBC Television's landmark history series *In Search of Scotland*.
304pp 100 illus. Paperback
£9.99/$14.99   ISBN 0 7524 2331 2

The Kings & Queens of Scotland
Richard Oram (Editor)
'the colourful, complex and frequently bloody story of Scottish rulers... an exciting if rarely edifying tale, told in a clear and elegant format.'
BBC History Magazine
'remarkable' *History Today*
272pp 212 illus (29 col) Paperback
£16.99/$22.99   ISBN 0 7524 1991 9

UK ORDERING

Simply write, stating the quantity of books required and enclosing a cheque for the correct amount, to: Sales Department, Tempus Publishing Ltd, The Mill, Brimscombe Port, Stroud, Glos. GL5 2QG, UK.

Alternatively, call the sales department on 01453 883300 to pay by Switch, Visa or Mastercard.

US ORDERING

Please call Arcadia Publishing, a division of Tempus Publishing, toll free on 1-888-313-2665